BASIC BOOK OF FLOWER GARDENING

IN THE SAME SERIES

Vegetable Growing
Rock Gardens and Pools
Chrysanthemum Growing
Rose Growing
Dahlia Growing
Decorative Shrubs
Herbaceous Borders
Pruning Trees, Bushes and Shrubs

OTHER TITLES IN PREPARATION

BASIC BOOK OF FLOWER GARDENING

W. E. SHEWELL-COOPER

MBE, NDH, FLS, FRSL, Dip.Hort.(Wye), DLitt

BARRIE & JENKINS

COMMUNICA - EUROPA

© W. E. Shewell-Cooper 1972, 1976

Second edition published 1976
by Barrie & Jenkins Ltd,
24 Highbury Crescent, London N5 1RX

ISBN 0 214 20140 6

Printed
in Great Britain by
BIDDLES LIMITED
Guildford, Surrey.

Contents

Illustrations Black and white photographs and line drawings

Colour Illustrations

*This young visitor to Arkley Manor believes in admiring
the flower beds at close quarters.*

DEDICATED TO MY FRIEND
Sir Emrys Jones, B.Sc.,
Director-General of the A.D.A.S. of The Ministry of Agriculture, Fisheries and Food, who has greatly encouraged me in my work.

Preface

This present work is a companion to my 'Basic Book of Vegetable Growing' and like it is intended as a guide for beginners. So please do not expect to find in it everything that could possibly be written about flowers!

A far greater interest is certain to be taken in flower gardening over the next few years. I hope this means that we shall have bigger and brighter herbaceous borders, lovely natural drifts of annuals, and masses of beautiful flowering shrubs which give so little trouble.

I should like to thank Tom Stacey Ltd. for the interest they have taken not only in this book but all the titles of this gardening series. This is indeed a team book and I should like to thank the Staff of the International Horticultural Advisory Bureau for all their help, for instance, Miss Gweneth Wood, Dip.Hort. (Swanley), Miss Margaret Call, Dip.Hort. (Studley) and my son, Mr. C. R. G. Shewell-Cooper.

I always like to receive letters from readers. Thousands have come in as a result of the many books on gardening I have written. So don't be afraid of sending in helpful suggestions so that we can make the next edition of this book even better than this one.

We gardeners have the reputation of helping one another. Let us continue this by passing on our treasured hints and tips to others. Fellows of the Good Gardeners' Association are very co-operative in this way. I would therefore be so glad to make you a Fellow too!

W. E. SHEWELL-COOPER,

The International Horticultural Advisory Bureau,
Arkley, Herts.

1 The Wonder of Growing Flowers

Flower gardening is a fascinating hobby and one which can give a tremendous amount of pleasure for a comparatively little outlay. The annual border is cheap. It is just a few pennyworth of flower seeds. The rose garden is inexpensive. You buy roses and they last for 10 years and more, so even if you pay 38p per bush it only works out at 3.8p per year! The same holds good for the shrub border. This is a permanent feature and the money you spend on it cannot be debited to one year only. Even the herbaceous border will last for 4 or 5 years, and then when you dig it up and split your plants you will be able to plant several other herbaceous borders or supply your friends and neighbours. So let us away with the idea that flower gardening is expensive. The beauty it provides may make all the difference to your mental outlook, for it will cater adequately for your aesthetic sense.

The great thing about the flower garden is that it must be your own. A book like this is only intended to give ideas. The keen gardener will want to interpret his own ideas. He may change them in years to come, but when he starts he should study first a book of this kind, and then having absorbed all he can, should put into practice what he feels will best interpret his desires. Personally, I hate the garden that is just a copy of another. It is seldom that the copyist succeeds. For what suits one piece of land or one district or one's house does not necessarily fit in with the general outline of another house and another area.

The flower garden should never be a burden, and there are so many facets to this delightful occupation that the busy man or woman must concentrate on the kinds of flower growing which take little time. The rose garden for instance is comparatively simple to care for; a well-planned herbaceous border with perennials planted in it that need no staking, is a boon to the week-end gardener. The sowing of the annual border and the necessary thinning and staking ensures rather too much work for the person with few hours to spare. Spring, summer and autumn bedding, though beautiful, take a good deal of time, but the joy of flower gardening is that you, the garden owner, may choose, you may decide what you will have – it will be your garden!

If there is to be joy in this flower garden of yours, see to it that you have flowers all the year round. By studying garden catalogues, by reading the chapters that follow, by talking about the matter with experts, you will soon find how you may have Christmas roses, autumn flowering crocus, winter flowering jasmine, late blooming Michaelmas daisies. You will look for January and February blossoms on your shrubs. You will find joy in the little winter aconites as they peep through. You will have some bulbs in bowls for indoors, and so the 'colourful joy' will continue.

There are far too many gardens today that look grand in June and July, and then are most disappointing in September and October, and there is no need for this. If there is any joy in growing flowers, as the chapter heading suggests, it is in being able to have them all the year round and with one or two aids, like continuous cloches, or a cold frame, this is a solid possibility. There are some who take a pride in wearing a good buttonhole every day of the year, and one which they actually pick from their own garden in the open.

Lastly, do look at Chapter 9 before you go much farther. How easy it is to be so proud of your flowers outside that yon never allow anyone to cut a bunch or two for decoration in the house. I can sympathize with the man who comes home after a hard day's work and finds that his wife has robbed his herbaceous border of 50 per cent. of its beauty, but that robbery would not have been necessary had there been a special part of the garden, however small, devoted to rows of flowers grown specially for cutting purposes.

My wife and I find this the ideal method. It is the perfect compromise. A great deal of joy is given to those who come to our home by the tastefully arranged bowls and vases which are to be seen in the living rooms of the house.

2 The Basis of a Good Flower Garden

No one would dare build a beautiful house today without good foundations and yet, again, attempts are made to produce magnificent flowers without giving the right attention to the foundation – the soil. Before starting on any planting scheme, the soil should be given every attention. There may be the necessity for drainage. There certainly will be a great need for digging in organic matter. There will be a lime requirement, but, of course, not in the area to be planted up with plants like Rhododendrons, that dislike lime.

Get to know your soil! Do not regard it as only containing disintegrated rock or minerals. It contains also certain quantities of organic matter, living organisms, moisture and 'gasses'. Usually speaking, the top 8 or 9 inches will be dark in colour due to organic matter and to oxidization, and the soil below, lighter.

Much has been done by all types of so-called agents to build up the substance we now know as soil. Wind has transported matter from a distance. Rivers have carried down silt. Glaciers in the past have worn down rocks to the finest powder. Burrowing animals have played their part, while the earth worms have done a great work not only by bringing portions of subsoil to the surface, but also by pulling down dead leaves and other decaying vegetable matter into the ground below.

Lots of plant roots in the past have penetrated the soil and aerated it. Soil bacteria by the million have worked on the organic matter and have initiated the formation of humus. Even ants have helped, and many a gardener has found the ant heap ideal for making seed beds when mixed with a little sand, even though he has not wanted them in his flower border or in his 'ports'!

Which of these five classes of soil does yours most resemble? The clays, the sands, the loams, the limey or calcareous soils, and the peaty or moss lands. A clay soil is silky and smooth to the touch, and even when well-drained it is apt to be wet. It is difficult to cultivate during wet periods, for if it worked at this time it may settle down like cement. Clay soils may have to be shallowly dug in the autumn and left so that the frost can somewhat pulverize them, and then, they are more easily workable in the spring. Clay soils need lime, for this helps to open them up and prevents them from becoming too sticky. Don't despise the clay, however, for it will be much richer in plant food than a sandy soil, and in a dry season will have far better water retention properties. A clay can do with having plenty of powdery compost or sedge peat forked into it lightly.

A sand is light and dry, easy to cultivate, and can be worked at any time of the year. It is unusually poor in plant foods and in organic matter, and every year large amounts of well-rotted powdery compost should be forked in to keep up the humus content. Sands are poor in plant foods, especially potash, and they may be acid and need lime.

Loams have been said to be the ideal blend of sand and clay; they should have the advantages of the two and none of their disadvantages. Loams may differ in accordance with the proportions of sand and clay present.

Calcareous or limey and chalky soils lack humus and plant foods. Like clays they are often difficult to work in rainy periods and in the summer they generally suffer from lack of water. Plants growing on chalky soils often suffer from Chlorosis; that is, the leaves go yellow and the growth is often stunted. A great improvement can be effected if a large amount of properly prepared compost is forked in each year.

Peaty soils are sour. They are often waterlogged and may need draining. They have, however, plenty of organic matter present. The brown peats are preferred to the black peat.

The Wheel of Life

Nature's plan is to build up the humus year after year and this can only be done by organic matter. There is need to replace and return that which has been taken out. The Chinese, who are the best gardeners, collect, 'use', and return to the soil, every possible kind of waste, vegetable, animal and human. In over 4,000 years of intensive cultivation they still support more human beings per acre than any other country in the world! On the other hand in areas like the Middle West of the U.S.A. and the Regina Plain of Canada, where the Wheel of Life has not been recognized, tens of thousands of acres which once grew heavy crops are now useless, or practically so.

Every flower crop grown reduces the organic content of the ground. Every piece of work done helps to break down the humus. The value of the soil in your garden, therefore, is not the mica particles or grains of sand. It lies in the humus that the soil contains. Humus makes all the difference to successful gardening. Have plenty of humus present and the soil is in good tilth. Humus is the organic colloid of the soil. It can store water, it can store plant foods, it can help to keep the soil open. It can help to ensure the right aeration. It will give ideal insulation against heat and cold.

Using Compost. Garden owners proposing to dig their land shallowly in preparation for flower growing, should realize the importance of adding ample quantities of organic matter before they start. Composted farmyard manure, fine wool shoddy, properly composted vegetable refuse, or hop manure should be added at the rate of one good barrow-load to 12 sq. yards and in addition into the top 1 or 2 in. of soil finely divided sedge peat, non-acid in character should be raked in at about half a bucketful (2 gal.) per sq. yard. This organic matter in the top few inches of soil gives the little roots a good start and so sends them on to find the organic matter below. (See *Compost* below.)

It is when the organic content of the soil has been helped in this way, that the gardener dares to add plant foods of an organic origin. These are usually applied on the surface of the ground and raked in. Fertilizers with an organic base are particularly useful. Fish Manure may be applied at 3-4 oz. to the sq. yard, or a meat and bone meal or even hoof and horn meal mixed with equal quantities of wood ashes may be used at a similar rate. These plant foods can be supplied not only when the flower garden is first made but every season very early in the spring. A good dried poultry manure to which a little potash has been added is another fertilizer that is very useful when applied at this time.

Minimum Digging. Flower growers must realize that proper soil treatment is the first essential to success. The millions and millions of soil bacteria that live in the ground to help the gardener, much appreciate little or no digging. It enables them to work better, for they need conditions which are natural. So do give them what they need.

Liming. Lime should be regarded as an essential except in very definite cases where acidity is demanded, e.g. the heaths and heathers, rhododendrons and azaleas.

Lime not only prevents soil from being acid but it 'sweetens' it, as well as playing its part as a plant food. It improves the texture and workability of heavy soils. It helps to release other plant foods, and it decomposes organic compounds in the soil so that they can be used as plant food also.

Generally speaking it should be applied at about 7 oz. to the sq. yard. It should not be dug in, as it washes down into the soil very quickly. It should be sprinkled on the surface of the ground after the digging and manuring has been done. Do not mix lime with organic fertilizers. There are three main types of lime : Quicklime, sometimes sold as Buxton Lime or Lump Lime, which has to be slaked down on the soil; Chalk or Limestone often sold as Ground Limestone, only half as valuable as quicklime; and Hydrated Lime, which is perhaps the most convenient to handle and is therefore most usually used by gardeners. The quantity of lime mentioned previously, i.e. 7 oz. per sq. yard, refers to hydrated lime.

Compost. 'Everything that has lived can live again in another plant' – this is the law of return sometimes called the 'Complete Cycle'. Thus, those who want to grow the best flowers, blossoms with perfect colouring, blooms with the maximum of scent, flowers that last well in water, must realize the importance of making perfect compost and then giving this blackish-brown powdery substance to the flower borders as a mulch.

I used to teach that deep digging was necessary for first-class results, but I have not dug any soil for flowers for some 15 years now and each year I get better results. The compost that is made goes as a 1 in. layer all over the soil and the worms pull it in and so build up the humus content of the soil. They do the digging for the garden owner by providing the air channels down which the air, moisture and plant foods can go.

Even in the case of soils where there seems to be no worms, there will be worm capsules which will soon hatch out into worms. These creatures hate to multiply in dug ground and they cease to function in land that is regularly fed with chemical fertilizers. The millions of living organisms that Nature has provided to work in the earth in order to produce plant foods and humus do not like being disturbed either. They mostly live in the top 3 or 4 inches of soil and they obviously dislike being buried by those who insist on the old-fashioned bastard trenching and the like.

Modern successful organic flower growing, therefore, relies on the worms, the bacteria and beneficial fungi to deal with the soil cultivation and aeration, and they, in consequence, use the compost on top of the ground. Where they cannot make enough compost for one reason or another, medium grade sedge peat is used instead. This is Nature's own compost made from the sedges and rushes and the activator was the manure from the birds and animals.

Placing the sedge peat or compost on top of the soil smothers the annual weeds and prevents them from growing and thus there is no hoeing to do at all. It is *not* necessary to put fresh compost on the soil each year. The flower beds in my garden at Arkley Manor have not been touched for 10 years. The compost is in position and stays there acting as a weed suppressor and a mulch to keep the moisture in the soil. Diseases are controlled in this way also and the beds themselves look extremely attractive with a lovely dark brown covering all over them.

The Compost Heap

A bin should be made with planks of wood so that there are 1 in. spaces between them. The bin must be square, either 4 ft by 4 ft, 6 ft by 6 ft, or, in big flower gardens, 8 ft by 8 ft. The wood of this bin should be treated with Rentokil to prevent the wood rotting away. There should be no wooden base because when the vegetable waste is put into the bin the worms must be able to work their way up into the bin and carry out their important work.

All the living material whatever it may be is put into the bin, mixing, if possible, the tougher waste with the softer matter like lawn mowings. The waste bin must be kept level all the time and the gardener should tread on the organic waste from time to time to keep it fairly compact and firm.

For every 6 in. thickness of waste collected, an activator must be given. This is to feed the bacteria and encourage them to work. Use dried powdered poultry manure, fish manure, seaweed manure, meat and bone meal, rabbit droppings, pigeon manure – on the basis of about 3 oz. to the sq. yard. In the trials at the Experimental Gardens of The Good Gardeners' Association at Arkley, the seaweed fertilizer has given the best results during the first few years.

When the bin is full, i.e. has risen to a height of, say, 6 ft, a 1 in. layer of soil should be placed all over the top so as to help conserve the heat in the heap. Those who cannot bother to throw soil on to the heap may cover it instead with a couple of blankets or even an old carpet.

At the end of six months, if the heap has been properly made layer by layer, and has been correctly activated, all the vegetable waste should have rotted down to a brownish-black powder. All the weeds will have been killed as well as all the pests and diseases. The brown compost will contain all the necessary plant foods known as macro-nutrients as well as the micro-nutrients which are so important, AND, what is even more important, the vitamins, enzymes and anti-biotics which will make all the difference to successful flower growing.

As the compost takes 6 months to mature from the time the bin is full and capped, it is advised to make 2 compost bins, the one next to the other. Thus, while Bin No. 1 is ripening, Bin No. 2 can be filled gradually.

Remember the slogan 'Everything that has lived can live again in another plant'. This means what it says. Don't therefore, believe old-fashioned gardeners who say 'Don't put sycamore leaves on the compost heap – or rhubarb leaves, laurel leaves, ivy leaves' – or whatever the 'old wives' tale' has suggested. All leaves make good compost, as do coffee grounds, tea leaves, banana peel, the cut-down perennials, the annuals when pulled up and, of course, the lawn mowings. By the way, the mowings alone can settle down too tightly and thus the air cannot get in between and so the 'good' bacteria cannot breathe. The result is that the anaerobic bacteria take over and putrefaction takes place. So make the layers of lawn mowings only two inches thick and level and lay on top of them 2 flat sheets of newspaper. Then put on another 2 in. layer of lawn mowings, next another layer of newspapers, and so on. The result will be that the paper will ensure that the air circulates among the grass clippings and thus they rot down properly.

The keen flower grower will collect all the organic matter he can from the kitchen of his home as well as from the garden and, maybe, from the local greengrocer's shop, who will be glad to give a weekly sackful or two of vegetable waste to a keen composter, and thus save having to put it in the dustbin. It is surprising what can be collected from the trees in the avenue – from the local barber (for hair makes good compost) – from the neighbour next door who is not garden-minded and so on.

Anyway, it can be said that properly-made compost is the secret of successful flower growing with the minimum of work. Where home-made compost cannot be or is not made, medium grade sedge peat can be used instead – for this is indeed Nature's compost.

The Use of Fertilizers

There are some who have said that in time artificial fertilizers will be used to replace organic manures entirely. Practical gardeners, however, know that humus is all important, and that if the culture of plants is to be kept at a high level and the soil improved, then the application of compost or organic manures is an absolute necessity; but that organic fertilizers can be used in addition to meet the plant's extra requirements. Once the compost has been provided then the organic fertilizer can play a part in stimulating crops.

Organic fertilizers can be roughly divided into three groups, nitrogen, phosphates and potash. Each has a part to play in building up perfect flowers. These three main plant foods should be present in the right proportions. They are (1) Nitrogen, which has to do with the building up of the stems and green leaves of the plant. It is when, however, too much nitrogen is given all the energies of the plant may be directed towards rank shoots and leaves, with the result that its floriferousness is impaired. (2) Phosphates which mainly affect the root growth and help to hasten earlier flowering, giving steady, firm continuous growth, and (3) Potash which plays an important part in the production of sturdy firm plants with blooms of a better colour, and it is said a better scent. Plants grown without sufficient potash may have softish leaves that easily succumb to disease.

The Organic Fertilizers Available. *Nitrogenous.* Dried Blood is the commonest organic fertilizer supplying nitrogen only. It is rather expensive and is used at 2 oz. to the sq. yard as a rule. Soot is the alternative – preferably old soot – and used at 3-4 oz. to the sq. yard.

Phosphates. Bone meal is the organic fertilizer most

used. It supplies phosphates slowly. It is usually used at 3-4 oz. to the sq. yard. Steamed Bone Flour is sometimes applied at 3 oz. to the sq. yard. It is very slow in action and so its use is generally restricted to the permanent crops like shrubs, roses and perennials.

Potash. Wood Ashes are almost the only natural form of potash. They are applied at 6-8 oz. to the sq. yard generally speaking. N.B. It used to be possible to obtain potash made from grape skins in quite large quantities. It is hoped that this organic fertilizer will be available again.

Compound Organic Fertilizers. *Fish Manure.* Usually contains 5% nitrogen and 6% phosphates and sometimes 6% of added potash in the form of flue dust or the like.

Hoof and Horn Meal. Contains 4% of Nitrogen only and this is released slowly.

Blood and Fish Bone. Contains 5% of Nitrogen, 9% Phosphates, and 5% Potash. This is well balanced organic fertilizer for the flower grower.

Seaweed Fertilizer. Is low in the macro-nutrients probably 1% Nitrogen, 1% Phosphate and 1% Potash but it contains an abundance of the micro-nutrients.

Fortified Seaweed Fertilizer. Is far richer in plant foods – the analysis being 6% Nitrogen, 7% Phosphates, and 4% Potash plus of course the micro-nutrients. It is deservedly very popular.

Paths have been described as a necessary evil. On the
other hand the great Diarist, Pepys, had a great admira-
tion for paths and lawns, and did not care for flower beds.
To enjoy a garden – and that is what a garden is for –
there must be paths, along which the wheelbarrow can
trundle, for though the wheelbarrow is no thing of beauty,
it is an absolute necessity at certain seasons of the year.
There will be paths needed for the mower, from the tool-
shed to the lawn, and of course, there is nothing like a good
path for strolling down on a summer evening to introduce
your friends and neighbours to the magnificent blooms
that you have produced. The great thing to realize is that
paths are necessary to get from one part of the garden to
another, but to make the garden a mass of paths is a great
mistake.

*It is always useful to have a seat where you can sit
quietly and enjoy your garden.*

As a rule, houses are built with right-angles and it is
very simple by extending the lines of the house walls, to
arrange right-angled paths. Further paths may be necessary leading away to a lily pool or running through a rose
garden. The place for the paths will soon be discovered,
once the plan has been prepared, even though this be in
rough. Having pegged out the beds and borders the paths
must be made first, for you cannot use the barrow com--
fortably until the path is there. There is no need, however,

to complete the whole path, providing you put in the foundations. You can always leave the surface dressing till the last. Ornamental paths and all main paths for egress and access, should be 4 ft wide to allow two people to walk abreast or to pass one another. Service paths as they are called, which lead through to the rock garden or lily pool need only be 2 ft wide and are usually 'winding'.

It is impossible to make a good path without excavation, for ample drainage must always be provided. Dig out the soil to a depth of 9 in. in the case of light land and 1 ft in the case of heavy soil, throwing the top spit on to the border alongside, but carting the bottom spit away to another part of the garden where it may be used as a foundation for, say, a rock garden.

Next spread a 6 in. layer of broken brickbats, coarse large stones, cinders, old iron, etc., in the bottom. If you use old tins, these should be beaten flat. It is upon this thick layer of material that a 4 in. depth of coarse gravel should be placed. 1 cubic yard of this is necessary for each 9 sq. yards of path to be laid down. Over the coarse gravel should then be placed the 2 in. of whatever surfacing material is to be used. It may be fine gravel. It may be cinders, or even tar macadam. See that the path is not dead level. There should be a camber of about $1\frac{1}{2}$ in. to the 4 ft walk, and about $\frac{3}{4}$ in. to the 2 ft walk. Well roll each layer as it is spread into position and if the paths have to be made during a dry period, use plenty of water between each rolling. By doing this a really firm foundation is assured. Gravel paths can be tarred over or covered with one of the more bituminous compounds. They are then easier to keep clean.

Paths

Concrete Paths. A concrete path is clean and very durable. The soil should be removed to a depth of 2 in. and a 2 in. or so foundation of gravel or stone should be laid down. Strong pieces of wood 2 in. in depth should then be laid down alongside the edge of the path, with pegs driven in to keep this wood in position. These strips hold the concrete up while the path is being made. On a clean stone or wood floor, mix up the cement to a formula of 3 buckets of shingle, 2 buckets of sand and 1 bucket of cement. Mix the sand and cement first by turning them over and over 3 times. Then add the shingle, and repeat the process.

PATHWAYS

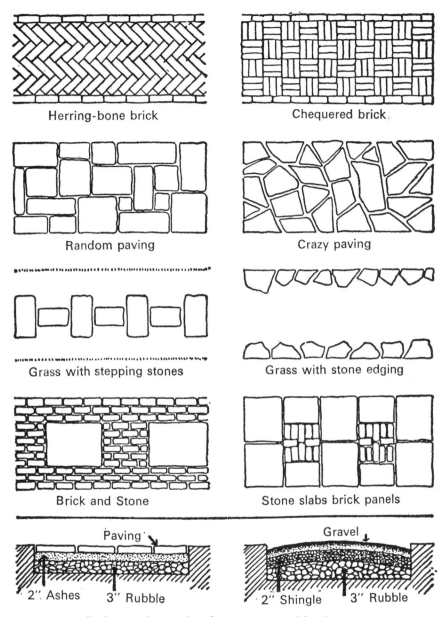

Herring-bone brick

Chequered brick

Random paving

Crazy paving

Grass with stepping stones

Grass with stone edging

Brick and Stone

Stone slabs brick panels

Paving

2" Ashes   3" Rubble

Gravel

2" Shingle   3" Rubble

Paths can be made of one or a combination
of several different materials.

Lastly add the water, and for the quantity mentioned not more than three-quarters of a two gallon bucket full will be required. Add this water gradually, turning all the time.

Water the surface where the concrete is to be laid. Do not put too much concrete down at a time, and level off by working a piece of wood forward over the surface. It is easy to do this if the two sides of the wood rest on the wooden edges of the path. Prevent the new concrete from drying out too quickly by covering the path when laid with damp sacks. One bag of cement, 2½ cubic ft of sand and 3¾ cubic ft of shingle will make enough concrete to lay a path down 2 ft wide, 2 in. thick and 15 ft long.

Crazy Paths. Some people prefer crazy paving or flag paths and these are quite suitable for a formal garden, and around a certain type of house. Do not, however, just lay the crazy paving or flag stones direct on to the soil. Make the necessary foundation as advised for the gravel path, but instead of using the gravel put 4 in. of the original top fertile soil under the paving stones so that rock plants may be made to grow in between. If the soil is mixed with a certain amount of sand better drainage is assured. Crazy paving and flag stones should be laid with a straight edge as this is the only way of ensuring that the surface is level and smooth. Unevenly laid stones may be dangerous. Do not use cement between all the cracks. These cracks are much better furnished with alpine plants. If you must use cement, because you fear an awful lot of weeding, then leave cracks here and there for the plants, and the whole effect will be far more natural.

Grass Paths. A grass path looks well, providing it is not worn down the centre (as it so often is) or ruined at one end. Such paths are not hard wearing and are not at all suitable for barrowing on. Pay great attention to the drainage when making grass paths and either lay down turves, packing all the joints with finely prepared soil mixed with a little grass seed, or sow the natural surface soil with a good lawn seed (preferably not containing perennial rye grass) at the rate of 3 oz per sq. yard. If you sow a path down with grass seed you will not be able to use it for three months or so.

Brick Paths. Old bricks are quite suitable for making paths providing they are not the kind which crumble during frosty weather. It is possible with bricks to make an

infinite number of patterns in the path, and a well pat-
terned pathway adds to the interest of the garden, especially in the winter. A good foundation should be prepared

BRICK EDGES TO PATHS ——

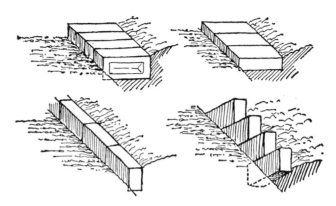

as for the gravel path, and the bricks may be laid down
lengthwise on cinders or sand. Some people prefer to lay
them on a cement foundation, and then they lay a certain

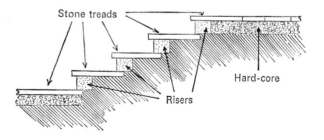

Steps with gravel treads supported by wooden edgings

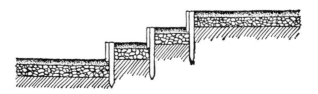

amount of cement between the joints. To obtain the true
cottage garden effect, *no* cement should be used between
the bricks.

Edging the Paths. Grass paths need no special edging. The edging is done with a turf cutter once or twice a year if necessary, or the grass is cut back with a pair of long-handled shears. Crazy and flagstone paths do not need any edging either. Sometimes informal grass paths can be edged with crazy paving so as to obviate the need of using edging tools and to allow almost the whole of the grass path to be cut with the ordinary mower. In this case the 'edging slabs' should be laid with their straight edges along the side of the border. Brick paths need no raised edges, but sometimes bricks are used on end or at a slant of about 45 degrees as an edging to a cinder or gravel path.

One of the most satisfactory methods of edging a path is by means of concrete. A narrow concrete edge need only be raised 2 in. above the path level and it is not difficult to run this in, in situ, between two boards laid edgewise along the path. The concrete for this should be made with one part cement and three parts sand. To make the concrete less obvious it is possible to paint the edging with a strong solution of iron sulphate crystals in water, and the edging will then turn a pleasing dull brown colour. The 'paint' can also be used for concrete paths to make them less glaring.

Walls

Here reference is made to garden walls – the type that can be used for growing plants between the bricks or stones, not ordinary brick walls that may divide one garden from another. Walls are sometimes necessary to act as retainers between two different levels of the garden and serving to hold the soil in place. Such a retaining wall has only one face. Terraces are often formed with retaining walls of this type. Walls are also sometimes used as low partitions between one part of the garden and another. Partition walls are double faced. These are far more uncommon on the whole than retaining walls.

Informal retaining walls can be made of limestone, sandstone, flints, bricks and large cobbles. It takes about one ton of such material to build 4 sq. yards of wall 'face'. Having obtained the necessary quantity of wall material, the soil should be piled to the desired shape. It should tilt backwards slightly at about 1½ in. to each foot. A 4-ft retaining wall, for instance, should have a slight tilt backwards of about 6 in. Retaining walls are always built from the bottom upwards; each stone should be absolutely firm, and plenty of soil should be rammed in between the stones and behind them to keep them in place. Every now and then a piece of rockery stone should be allowed to go back well into the soil at the back so as to give strength to the whole structure. Here and there a little space should be left between the stones and the soil not rammed in too tightly, so that any excess moisture may drain through.

Most retaining walls are planted up with alpines, and nurserymen can provide flowering plants specially suited for the purpose. These include : Wallflowers, Pinks, Centranthus, Antirrhinums, House Leeks (sempervivums), Arabis, Aubrietia, Campanulas, Corydalis, Iberis sempervirens, Silene schafta, Alyssum saxatile, Erinus alpinus, Saponaria ocymoides, Sedums, Thymus nitida.

The planting can be done as the wall-making proceeds. Where plants cannot be obtained, the sowing of seeds is the alternative, and the secret of success is to mix the seeds into balls of soil first and then to press these into the cracks in between the stones. The top of a retaining wall is usually planted with dwarf shrubs or with bedding plants, such as wallflowers and forget-me-nots for the spring and antirrhinums or dwarf dahlias for the summer.

Division walls are made in a similar manner and can be extremely ornamental. They should always slope to the top so that the bottom is wider than the apex. The part between the two wall faces should be filled with good soil and there should be a space of 8 in. at the top for the plantings of flowers such as antirrhinums, valerian, wallflowers and the like. Do not have the top of the wall set with pointed rocks that look like dragon's teeth. The top of a divisional wall should always be flat.

4 Stocking Up

Herbaceous Plants

Buying plants is a fairly simple matter and I shall deal with that in detail later on. But there are hundreds of kindly disposed garden owners who are only too glad to give small pieces of perennials to those who are starting *de novo* or even to friends who are short of a particular variety or type. In some districts, garden Clubs or Societies arrange for the exchange and distribution of herbaceous plants in the winter time. Under such circumstances there is no begging in that sense of the word. It is a gift gladly given.

There is always a danger, however, in accepting roots of herbaceous flowers from wellwishers. It is invariably the rampant grower that can be most easily spared because it spreads prodigiously. Accept with care then, those bits and pieces which are so often offered lavishly by those who ought to know better! Find the true name of what is being offered to you. Look up the plant in a catalogue or encyclopaedia, or even better if you can see how it is growing for yourself, in the garden of the owner who has made you such a 'kind' offer.

Rampant Flowers

I should like, therefore, to warn you against a few which have what I call 'Wanderlust'. They are all right if they can be kept in order, but can you guarantee to do this? They may find a niche in a very large garden. The plants are in no particular order but just as they come to mind. The list is a warning in itself.

Thermopsis montana. Travels subterraneously for yards.

Physalis alkekengi. The Chinese Lantern flower – and what a spreader!

Campanula persicifolia. Throw too few flowers.

Polygonum cuspidatum. Spreads and spreads like mad.

Petasites fragrans Winter heliotrope. Deliciously scented in January, but its large leaves smother the ground later on and exclude other plants.

Cerastium tomentosum. Rhizomes will penetrate anywhere and ruin a rock garden.

Euphorbia cyparissias. Cypress spurge. Spreads with thread-like roots which are very difficult to eradicate.

Centranthus ruber. Such a nuisance because it seeds itself badly.

Oenothera biennis. The Evening Primrose, another one which flings seeds about everywhere.

Linaria cymbalaria. Another trailing spreader which seeds prolifically.

Anemone japonica. Beautiful, though it can become a perfect menace.

These plants will serve to show what I mean. Beware of them as well as some of the very common rampageous Michaelmas daisies, which seem to spread like couch grass and pop up at unexpected places.

The Right Time. Another mistake that is so often made in begging is that the plants are given – or rather the portions thereof – at the wrong time. Most herbaceous plants do best when put into the new borders early in the autumn. There are exceptions to the rule, and it can be said, where gardens are situated in smoky towns or cities, that March planting is to be preferred. The great thing with spring planting is to make certain that the plants do not suffer from drought. They are planted late and have to grow, and flower, and form new roots at approximately the same time, and they cannot do this in dry soils. They are helped tremendously if they get a good mulching (this means top dressing) of damped sedge peat, well composted vegetable refuse or similar material. This is put around the plants in April or early May and acts as a barrier between the sunshine and the soil, keeping the moisture in below and incidentally providing the organic matter which is so much needed.

Perennial Weeds. Be very careful from whom you accept plants. Many gardeners have cursed the day when they received the gift, from a so-called friend, for within the clump or clumps so gladly provided there lay one of these insidious perennial weeds like convolvulus or ground elder. Once the plants are in position the weeds grow and before long the new garden owner is hard put to it to know what to do. It is always better to be safe than sorry. See the garden from which you will receive the plants and if there is any sign of perennial weeds about, say quite frankly, 'Thank you very much but I'm not having any!'

Buying the Best 'For me there is nothing better than the best.' That is a good motto to start with. Pay a fair price for a good article and be quite sure what you are buying. Do not try and buy clumps (though I have used that word when dealing with gifts). Remember that a clump is an old plant. Small pieces are what you need, a good vigorous young plant with a good root system. Buy a plant that will transplant well. You would not think of buying an old horse or an old cat. Don't therefore consider getting an old herbaceous perennial.

Remember that you yourself will be able to propagate many of the plants you buy in a year or two's time, so don't mind buying only ones or twos and thus have the joy of increasing your ones and twos to sixes and sevens. It is far better to pay say 30p or 40p for a really good worthwhile perennial than to pick up something in the cut-price stores at 10p per plant.

A large number of reliable nurserymen up and down the country can supply your needs. Write to them for a catalogue. Peruse this at leisure, making up your mind beforehand how much you can spend and then marking this plant and that plant until the sum you set aside has been expended. Some nurserymen specialize on certain types of flowers.

As a rule, at the start the flower grower will be content with getting all the plants he needs from some nursery on which he can rely, perhaps in the vicinity. He should go along and then see the plants blooming – not just one visit but a visit in July, another in August, and another in September, and so on, so that he covers the flowering periods of the season. On each occasion he can mark down in the catalogue the plants that he fancies and so his selection can be made from sight. Many parks have good herbaceous borders, with the plants well labelled. Regular visits will be well repaid. The Parks Superintendent or one of his assistants will often be willing to discuss perennials and their uses. Knowing the district, he may prove a valuable friend who can make helpful suggestions.

Flower growers who live in the south may like to visit the Royal Horticultural Society's Gardens at Wisley. Many go to the gardens of the Good Gardeners Association at Arkley Manor, Arkley, Nr. Barnet, Herts, and look at the plants in the big herbaceous borders there and in the cut flower borders. Those who are within reach of London will want to go to the fortnightly shows at the Royal Horticultural Society's Hall to see the flowers on display there, while those who live in the north may go to their Northern Flower Shows like those at Harrogate, Altrincham, the

Roundhay Show at Leeds and so on. Those hardy border plants are going to cost you money. So spend that money wisely and carefully, and know what you are buying very time.

Bulbs and Corms You will be lucky to get any bulbs and corms given you even if you beg for them! But the danger of a gift is of course disease, and for that matter, pests. Sometimes a nurseryman who forces flowers under glass is willing to give away or sell cheaply some of the bulbs after the cutting and marketing has been done. These often take years to recover from this treatment. They are grown for market, the foliage is often cut as well as the bloom and so there is little food to be passed back by the leaves into the bulb itself. Many would say that they are not worth anything at all, but I have known amateurs who have them and have planted them and nursed them, and in three or four years' time have got quite respectable blooms from them. It is a question of waiting.

When buying bulbs, you will do well to order them from a reliable seedsman and see that you are supplied with firm, good specimens at the right time.

Roses It is doubtful if anyone will have rose bushes to spare. The only time it is likely that they will be offered you as a gift is when someone is leaving the garden or when some estate is being broken up. In these cases the roses offered are invariably old and it is seldom they transplant well. My experience is that it is always better to plant a young rose bush with a really good root system, such as you can get from a first-class nurseryman.

Shrubs and Climbers Some amateurs are very keen on propagating shrubs and a number of shrubs can be raised from cuttings and seeds without much difficulty. It is not surprising to hear of garden owners who had little shrubs given to them from time to time but the danger of such gifts is threefold – (1) That you are given the most rampant plants which will take up a tremendous amount of room. (2) That you are given the very common varieties and types and (3) That you will be given those which are not so popular, perhaps. You want to be very careful in accepting such gifts. I know of a garden in Kent that accepted a gift of a plant twenty years

ago, and now it is the gardener's bane ! It has spread everywhere and the owner cannot even grow onions in the vegetable garden without it rearing its ugly head. Accept gifts,
therefore, with reservation. Make certain you know their
name, for instance, and then you can look the plants up
in a good shrub catalogue or in an encyclopaedia and see
what you are getting.

When buying shrubs, look out for a good root system.
Too many beginners want to buy a big top and that is a
great mistake. What you really want is a big bottom ! By
that I mean that the part below ground should be the part
that is really well developed. See that you buy young shrubs
because they more quickly acclimatize to your soil. Don't
ask for old ones. See that they come to you named and
be sure you make a plan or keep a list of the names because the labels soon get worn or tear off. Take a great
deal of trouble over buying and ordering shrubs. Buy those
that will not grow too large for your garden, that will need
little looking after, and that will give you colour over as
long a period as possible. In most gardens flowering shrubs
are preferable to a whole lot of evergreens.

5 The Ever-Popular Herbaceous Border

The herbaceous border is the most popular of all types of flower borders. It is so called because it is planted with herbaceous perennials, although today other types of plants, such as bulbs, are often included and so the border could easily be given a name as the Hardy Plant Border.

Such a border should be designed to cover as long a period of flowering as possible. The situation must be light and airy and away from the drip of trees. A southern aspect on the whole is best, though a northern aspect is quite possible. There must be protection from wind. If it is backed by a hedge – and such a background is excellent, then it is a good plan to have the border a little distance away. Use a hedge that will not compete with the flowers, one that has a quiet all-over tone like yew, Lonicera nidita or Thuya lobeii. A laurel hedge is bad, for the leaves are too big. It is often possible to use such a flower border to give an impression of length to the garden, especially where two borders run parallel side by side with, say, a 5 ft width of grass lawn between.

Part of Dr. Shewell-Cooper's herbaceous border, showing how successful his non-dig composting methods are.

The aspect of the border is important. It is such a nuisance to have planted the border and then find that the flowers solemnly turn their heads towards the sun and away from the house or path down which you walk. Remember that a newly planted border always looks a bit thin the first year but you cannot help that. You can always fill up the spaces the first season by sowing a few annuals in the spring.

Situation and Size

It has already been said that a southern aspect is best but, generally speaking, the herbaceous border will have to be fitted into the general layout of the garden, and as it will be planned in a long wide strip it should always be used to give an impression of length to the garden. This impression can be increased if a double herbaceous border with a wide grass path in between can be arranged. It is important to see that the borders and paths are in proportion in width and length. For instance, in a big garden the border if 200 yards long would look odd if it was only 6 ft wide. Under such circumstances it should be 15 ft wide. It is only in small gardens that a border can be as narrow as 4 ft and even then it is very difficult to make it look effective during all the summer months. A border 50 ft long should be 9 ft wide; 25 ft long should be 5 ft wide; 100 ft long, 12 ft wide, and so on.

Sometimes there is a double-fronted border – the herbaceous border with a grass verge or crazy paving on either side of it. The width of such a border again will depend on on the size of the garden and its length, and it will have to balance with the width of the path. Never make a border bigger than can be easily looked after. A well-kept herbaceous border is far more pleasurable than one which is not cared for properly even though it may be wider and longer.

Shape, Shelter and Background. A wall or hedge at the back of a herbaceous border gives the necessary shelter and background. A tall wall will, of course, give too much shade to a north border. On the other hand a south border with a wall behind is ideal, for the wall can be covered with the less rampant climbers, such as clematis and honeysuckle, and the general beauty is increased. A selection of clematis can ensure colour from May to October with the advantage that the roots are not soil robbers.

Normally hedges are used, especially evergreen ones, such as yew, a slow grower, and Lonicera nidita, a fast grower, which unfortunately may suffer from a hard winter in an exposed situation. Another good hedging plant for this purpose is Thuya lobbii. The difficulty here, however, is that the roots extend into the herbaceous border and rob it. For this reason some gardeners have taken the trouble to bury sheets of corrugated iron in the ground, perpendicularly, so as to restrict the roots to one side only.

The background, of course, might be a shrub border. It might consist of rambler roses trained on wires or a trellis. It might be formed of an undulating line of evergreen and flowering shrubs planted in such a way that the very tall herbaceous plants grew in the 'pockets' or bays thus formed by them. It is when the background is undulating that the front of the border might have gentle curves also. If, however, it is backed by a straight wall or hedge, the front of the border should be as straight as a die also. Incidentally this always adds a feeling of length.

Edgings. When the border has a grass path there will be no need to have a special edging. Each season the garden-line will be put down and the half-moon turfing iron used to ensure that it is absolutely straight. During the season

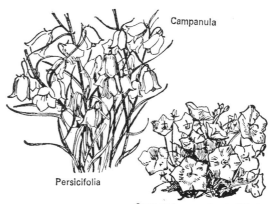

Campanula

Persicifolia

Campanula carpatica turibinata

Bleeding Heart   Dicentra spectabilis

a pair of long-handled shears will soon clip the edges. It is useful to have an 18-in. wide paving stone path arranged between the lawn and the border or to use a number of bricks laid flat to this width, instead. It so much depends on the house, which type fits best into the picture. The advantages are twofold − (1) the wheel of the mower can run along the paving without injuring the plants and so keep the lawn cut right to its edge and thus leave no untidiness. (2) The plants in the front of the border can tumble out naturally and thus break the hard lines without getting in the way of the mower or spoiling the grass. The latter trouble invariably occurs when the lawn goes right to the edge of the border.

Sometimes the path will be a gravel one or a modern bitumen one to give the same effect and in this case the edging will probably be brick or strips of concrete painted with ferrous sulphate to give them a weathered look.

Preparation of the Border

As a good perennial border may be down for eight years or so, much depends on the initial preparation. The normal forking over as advised in Chapter 2 will suffice but during this work the greatest care should be taken to get rid of any roots of perennial weeds. If the strip is very weedy it would be worth while to have potatoes on the land for a year, for this is an excellent cleaning crop and thus having waited a season you would know that final success was assured.

The shallow digging or forking should always be done early in the autumn to allow the soil to settle before planting begins. Into the top 2 or 3 in. should be forked sedge peat at a bucketful to the sq. yard. This will help to open up clay soils and provide the right medium for holding moisture in sandy soils. The tip is to use it dry with the clays and to damp it thoroughly before forking it into sandy soils. In addition, at the same time an organic fertilizer should be incorporated for this will release the plant foods slowly as the herbaceous flowers need them and also will provide material to help increase the humus content of the soil. All gardeners agree that it is soil texture that matters so much and everything should be done to improve the humus content by adding organic matter. Surface dressings of lime may have to be given on acid soils as advised in Chapter 2. This is particularly important in the case of clay soils whose mechanical condition is improved when its acidity is controlled by lime additons. But *never,* however, use lime where it is proposed to grow lime-hating plants.

Sometimes a herbaceous border has to be planted on a virgin soil. The new garden-owner finds that he has to start from scratch and this usually means digging in the grass. Never make the mistake of burning the turf. Either skim off the turf shallowly and stack it sprinkling fish manure in between the layers at 3 oz. to the sq. yard. In a year the turf should have turned into valuable 'manure'. It can then be spread over the border. The alternative is to rotovate the border mechanically or to fork over several times. The turf will then rot down and provide humus and food.

Do not worry too much if your soil is very stony. You cannot get rid of every stone you see and there is no need to. Stones improve aeration. They make the ground more porous and keep it cooler during hot periods. Of course when they are too numerous, as in a gravel soil, they do make for trouble and the best thing to do in such a garden is to dig in as much well-rotted organic matter as you can and to fork into the top 3 or 4 in. plenty of fine organic matter like sedge peat, even if you have to use it at a large bucketful per sq. yard.

Planning and Planting

I could very easily devote the whole book to the subject of planning. In fact I *have* devoted a whole book to the subject. Curiously enough no two people seem to agree and it is a good thing therefore that no one knows who is right! It is largely a question of taste. You may have two very good artists and they will dislike one another's work, so do not decry your own efforts at planning. It is your garden and you can have the border as you will. Let me, however, help you by mentioning one or two snags to look out for, and by making one or two suggestions which I think are worth following.

Succession. In the general herbaceous border for the ordinary garden, care should be taken to ensure that when one drift or clump of flowers fades, another one is coming along to take its place. If it can be arranged that this later flowering group is in front of the earlier flowering one, the cutdown stems of the latter will be hidden. When planning, think of times of flowering.

Height. Remember that some herbaceous flowers will grow

over 6 ft high and some only 9 in. The general rule will
be to keep the taller plants at the back of the border and
the dwarf ones towards the front. In a long border this
arrangement looks too formal if carried on right the way
through, and it is better every now and then to allow a
taller drift to come right to the front of the border and
thus break up the monotony.

COLOUR. Generally speaking, puce pinks should not be
planted next to bright reds. It is useful if plants with little
colour, those with greyish foliage and creamish flowers,
like Artemesia lactiflora for instance, can find themselves
next to the more dominant colours like red or bright blue.
It is useful if, in the drifts that are arranged, the lighter
blues can merge into the darker blues and on to the mauvy
blues at the back of the border. This quiet progression, from
one shade to another, delights the eye.

The garden artist will carry out the same kind of tech-
nique with the border as a whole, and will start for example
with the softer colours at one end of the border and the
brighter colours at the other end, or he may start with
softer colours at either end of the border and come to a
climax in the middle.

Other hints with regard to colour are : the mauve-pinks
do not like the bronzes; greys are always useful in that
they throw the brighter colours into relief. Blues and
mauves prefer contrasts and look well next to yellows and
and pale pinks; oranges like to be near other orange coloured flowers to look at their best. Strong yellows look well
with canopy bronzes and orange shades; while the light
yellows may be worked up well into oranges, scarlet and
crimson at the back of the border.

SHAPE. Some plants fall naturally into what I call the
spiky or spiry group like, for instance, delphiniums. Others
come into the bushy group, growing more like a big round
ball, like the feathery gypsophila. Do not have all the spiky
one together, nor equally, all the bushy ones in one place.
The plants will look at their best when they are mixed
together in their various shapes and forms. How important
it is to know as much as possible not only of the colour
and height but of the way the plant grows also. Much can
be learned from catalogues but more can be learned from
going to a good park and seeing the plants growing, or
visiting one of the gardens that are opened in aid of the

Queen's Nursing Funds like, for instance, Arkley **Manor**, Arkley, near Barnet, Herts.

Grouping or Drifting. There is nothing worse than **having** a border with different plants dotted about singly like **lone** sentinels. The narrow border should have clumps, or **drifts** as I prefer to call them, of 3 or 4, the wider border should have drifts of 6 or 7 plants, and the very wide 14 ft border **may** even have bigger groups than that. Don't plant **so** that the 4 or 5 lupins you put in are separated. Arrange **for** them to be in one group together, spaced at the right distance apart. You will be able to judge this by the height of the plant. Each of the lupins you plant will be **of the** same colour and shape and instead of planting them **in a** round or square clump you will arrange for them **to be in** a drift. They look more natural this way.

Eryngium

Echinops Ritro

Garden Cactus Dahlia

Prepare the border on paper first to make quite sure you are doing the right thing. I always use squared paper for the purpose and this makes it easier for me to work out the right distance apart the plants should be. You can then put little crosses on your plan showing where each plant is to grow and you can surround the drift the drift of each particular variety of plant with a pencil ring so that you see where you are going to as the plan proceeds, and so that you separate your groups and make it easier for you to transpose the plan on to the ground itself when planting time comes.

The Seasonal Border. It is possible to plan a herbaceous border for the spring only, say, to give you a show during March, April and May. This will have in it, for instance, doronicums and pæonies.

You can have a summer border which aims mainly to give a good show in June and July, especially if you take your holidays in August. The main features here would be lupins, iris and phlox. You may prefer to try an autumn border which is at its best in September and October and in this case you can concentrate on chrysanthemums, various types of Michaelmas daisies, dahlias and so on.

Single and Dual-coloured Borders. There are some folk who like a one-colour border and this is quite a possibility. Plant if you like, then, the all-blue border, the all-white border (which is particularly lovely at night). Then there are pastel shades – creamy-whites, pale yellows, feathery-whites with perhaps a touch of pink here and there. There are dual-coloured borders like red and yellow, or what might be called tripartite borders, such as blue, yellow and white. Normally, the beginner would do well to start with a mixed border which can look very beautiful at almost all times of the year.

In such a mixed border it is possible – though not advisable – to have a few roses, particularly China roses. Do not use rambler roses as a background for the border as they seldom fit it, particularly the pinks. If you must use a climber as a background to cover a trellis or whatever it may be, use ornamental vines which give colour in the autumn or various types of clematis.

If you are going to have bulbs in the border, plant them close to such plants as pæonies to avoid spearing them

PATH

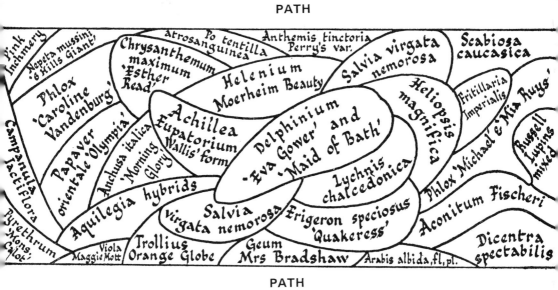

PATH

```
  1     2     3     4     5
```
cale ½″ to 1′

when you fork over the border in the late autumn or winter. Plant the bulbs deeply also for the same reason, i.e. about 9 in. deep.

General Planning Remarks Again I emphasize these points : (1) Think of flower shape contrasts – the featheriness of the gypsophila and the spiky tallness of the delphinium. (2) Remember the grey foliage plants. Pay attention to the appearance of plants in winter. (3) Don't forget the length of flowering period of each perennial you plant. (4) There is much to be said for the beauty of foliage as well as beauty of flower. (5) Some plants such as pæonies do not like being disturbed, and it is better to leave them down for 8 or 9 years; so plant them in a spot where they can remain even though the rest of the border is destined to be dug up and replanted every three years. (6) Some plants such as pyrethrum will flower twice a year. Remember to cut these down early so that they will flower again in the autumn. Make a note of this when you are planning. (7) Remember that blue gives an effect of distance, while reds and oranges and even bright yellows tend to bring things close. Therefore plant the blues away from the nearest viewpoint.

Pea sticks used for supporting border plants

It is not a simple matter to plan out a border, but the reader with realize that (a) no two people have the same taste and (b) what is poison to one is meat to another. Bear the points in mind that have been mentioned and then plan out your border boldly; as long as it satisfies you that is all that really matters. Suggestions have been given, and by studying catalogues and above all, by seeing what other people have done in their herbaceous borders you will be able to plant the border of your dreams.

Routine Work on an Established Border. Hoe the border* over regularly. Stake the plants early. Use the pea sticks as already advised pushed well in among the plants so that as they grow the sticks are covered up. Use bamboos only to stake tall plants such as delphiniums, and the height of the stake should be a few inches less than the height of the plant. The stakes should always follow the same lines as the plant according to their shape. Try not to use more than three bamboos to a plant, pushed in, say, at an angle of 60 degrees, tying green cotton twist or twill in between them to surround the plants. Such material does not show as obviously as does tarred string or raffia. It is made specially for the purpose.

Some plants flag badly in hot weather in light land. The tip here is to place empty flower pots sunk into the ground behind the plants and these may be filled up with water from time to time. The taller plants such as delphiniums and the bigger flowering plants such as pæonies appreciate feeds of liquid manure, which can be bought in bottles. Use it in accordance with the instructions on the label. Top dressings of compost should be given in May or early in June. These are known as mulches. They should be put on to a depth of 1-2 in. Medium grade sedge peat can be used instead. Don't forget to feed the plants that are to bloom twice in the season – catmint, lupins, and delphiniums for instance. This feeding should be done immediately after they have been cut down for the first time. Some plants, especially phlox, tend to send up rather weedy growth at the beginning of the year. If this is cut back, or cut out, it allows later growth to come up more strongly.

In the autumn, cut the flowering stems down to within 9 in. of the ground. Clear away all the old leaves and stems,

Border plants with long stems supported by bamboo and string

* No hoeing is necessary if you adopt the compost mulching system for the compost or sedge peat goes all over the soil 1 in. deep.

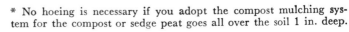

the pea sticks, bamboos and apply lime over and around the plants that need it, particularly the scabious and pyrethrum. Add at the same time powdery composted vegetable refuse or composted old manure at one bucketful per sq. yard if the worms have pulled some of the original mulch into the soil. Some perennials, particularly the Michaelmas daisies and the Chrysanthemum maximum, need dividing every other year. In the ordinary way the whole border will be lifted and replanted at the end of seven years, though gardeners who are energetic make up their minds to replant every five years.

Plants for a Herbaceous Border

In order not to make the book too technical, I have decided to give the plants one simple name and not attempt to muddle beginners with a whole lot of Latin "appendages."

It is impossible in a book of this size to include every plant that might be included in a herbaceous border, and so I have chosen those which any beginner may use with success – those that I have grown and know, and those which give a sufficiently broad picture from the point of view of height, colour, time of flowering and so on.

ACANTHUS. Has a rather unusual prickly flower. Grows 4 ft high with decorative leaves. Season, July-August. Likes full sun.

ACHILLEA. Often called the cultivated Yarrow. Flowers white, yellow or crimson. Dainty. Grows 2-4 ft high according to variety. My favourite, The Pearl, pure white double flowers.

ACONITUM. Often called Monkshood. Looks something like a delphinium, grows 3-6 ft high according to variety. Blue flowers. In season from July till September. My favourite, Spark's variety, a deep blue, 5 ft.

ALSTRŒMERIA. Often called the Peruvian Lily of the Incas. Has a thick fleshy root system. Often takes three years before it flowers properly. Height 2-3 ft. Its lily-like flowers are yellow and orange. Season, July. My favourite, Dover Orange, 2½ ft.

ALTHÆA. Commonly known as the Hollyhock. Grows 6-8 ft high bearing large single or double flowers coloured pink, white, apricot, cream, salmon or red. They are best treated as biennials because of the Rust Disease which ruins them after the first year or two.

ANCHUSA. A tall spreading plant with rough leaves and

smallish intense blue flowers. Has a deep rooting tap root. Grows 5 ft high. Season June-August according to variety. Likes a well-drained soil, therefore protect from excessive wet in winter. Can easily be propagated by root cuttings. My favourite, Morning Glory, because of its rich flowers borne in June and July.

ANEMONE. Sometimes called the Windflower. Tall branching stems 1½-3 ft high, bearing large single or semi-double showy 'mother-of-pearl' petal sheen type of flowers. These may be pink or white blooms from August till October. A tidy type of plant; likes semi-shade. Has been known to become a nuisance if it likes a soil, by spreading too much. My favourite, Lady Gilmour, which bears dark pink double flower in August on stems 2 ft high.

ANTHEMIS. The Chamomile. Bears single yellow flowers on stems 3 ft high from June till August. The greyish foliage is attractive. My favourite, Mrs. E. C. Buxton, a creamy yellow, in bloom June-August.

AQUILEGIA. Often called Columbine. A dainty plant with harebell-like flowers with tails to them. Often called longspurs. Should be grown in the middle of the border so that the plants in front can hide untidy stems and bare ground after flowering, which takes place from May-June. Height 1½-2½ ft according to variety. Likes full sun; does not divide well; usually last three in the border; raise some plants from seed each year. Can be had in innumerable delicate shades of many colours. My favourite, glandulosa, pure light blue 3 ft tall. Flowers June-July.

ARTEMESIA. The Wormwood. Chiefly grown for its grey feathery foliage. Flowers creamy white. In season in July and August. The plants always look tidy. My favourite, Lactiflora, a creamy-white, fragrant, summer flowerer, growing 5 ft tall.

ARMERIA. The Thrift. Makes a tufted plant out of which grows thin wiry stems bearing balls of pink or reddish flowers. Likes a well-drained soil with full sun. My favourite, Bees Giant Ruby.

ASTER. See Michaelmas daisies.

BOCCONIA. A tall imposing plant bearing golden feathery flower plumes and lovely greyey-bluish foliage. Height 6 ft. Useful from June -September. A gross feeder; can do with liquid manure weekly during the growing season. Can be a nuisance as it spreads so.

CAMPANULA. Commonly called the Bell-flower. A huge family whose plants flower in June and July though a few may extend till August. Height anything from 2-5½ ft, according to variety. Colour, white or blue. The plants like full sun but will do well in partial shade. A tidy grower. My favourite Telham Beauty, a pale blue, flowers in June, stems 3 ft high.

CATANANCHE. A delightfully neat plant whose flowers remind me of an everlasting cornflower – if there is such a thing. There is a deep blue, Cœrulea, and a white, Alba. They love full sun. They grow 2 ft high and flower from June till August.

CENTAUREA. The perennial Cornflower. Grows almost anywhere. Flowers may be blue, yellow, rose or white. Season, May and July-September. Grows 2-5 ft according to variety. C. macrocephala is a golden yellow, 4 ft. C. montana can be had in blue, pink or white, 1½ ft and C. dealbata, a pink, 2 ft.

CENTRANTHUS. Commonly called Red Valerian. Flowers in July with blooms on stems 1½ ft tall, either red or white. Loves a chalky soil.

CHRYSANTHEMUM MAXIMUM. Called the Ox-eyed Daisy or large marguerite. Grows 4½-5 ft tall according to variety. Large daisy-like flower with bright golden centre. In season June-October according to variety. There are varieties with frilled petals like Mrs. Collier, my favourite, Esther Read, a pure white double, 2 ft tall, flowers from July-September. (I have included the Moon Daisies C. uliginosum and the Ox-eyed daisies C. leucanthemum, etc., all under this heading. The half-hardy section usually described by amateurs as the true outdoor chrysanthemum, is dealt with in Chapter 14.)

COREOPSIS. Bears bright yellow daisy-like flowers from June-September on stems 2-3 ft high. Rather an untidy grower. My favourite, Sunburst, a double.

DELPHINIUM. One of the most beautiful herbaceous plants there is. A gross feeder and requires rich soil, manure and moisture. Michaelmas daisies are often planted in front to cover up the bare patches after the plants have been cut down. Height 3½-6 ft according to variety. Colour, every shade of blue, often with a touch of pink or mauve. There is a white variety now and a pink. Season, June-July. There are two distinct sections, the Elatum and the

Belladonna. The Elatum is the tall section and the Belladonna the group with plants of a dwarf or bushy habit,
valuable for planting towards the front of a border. My
favourite Belladonna is Peace, an intense blue; my favourite Elatum, Ann Page.

DIANTHUS. Commonly called pinks. A useful border
plant with grey-green spiky foliage. The pinks are usually
1 ft high and the border carnations 1½ ft. The pinks can be
had as whites or pinks and the border carnations in all
kinds of colours. My favourite pink is Mrs. Sinkins, a pure
double white of satin-like texture, and my favourite border
carnation, Beauty of Cambridge, a distinct pale yellow.
Pinks succeed in the coldest of soils; border carnations
require more drainage.

DICENTRA. Commonly called the Bleeding Heart. A
dwarf plant about 2 ft high with lovely ornamental foliage
and dainty heart-shaped pendant flowers. Bright pink.
Flowers from May till July. Likes liquid manure during
the growing season till the buds appear. Will grow in sun
or slight shade. Looks well with Solomon's Seal.

DORONICUM. Commonly called Leopard's Bane. Produces yellow daisy-like flowers from April to June on stems
1½-3 ft high according to variety. Will grow anywhere. Cut
back after flowering and the second crop will be produced
in late summer. My favourite, Harper Crewe.

ECHINOPS. Commonly called the Globe Thistle. Bears
thistle-like flowering balls blue in colour on stems 3-5 ft
tall from August till September. Look well near gypsophila.
My favourite, Ritro.

EREMURUS. Produces a tall majestic spike of flower 3-10
ft high according to variety. Flowers from May till July
with yellow, white or pink flowers according to variety.
These handsome plants need special care, but they are
gorgeous when well grown. They like rich soil, and they
hate disturbance. Protect during winter with bracken. My
favourite, E. Elwessianus, a pale pink, 10 ft. Give it a
sheltered position.

ERIGERON. Sometimes called Flea-bane. Bears pink,
mauve or purple daisy-like flowers with a yellow centre.
Grows 1-2½ ft tall and is in flower from May till August.
Must be well supported with pea sticks. My favourite,
Serenity, a violet blue, 2 ft.

ERYNGIUM. The Sea Holly. Bears thistle-like flower

heads, and has spiky foliage. Grows 2-4 ft tall with flowers and stems of a steely blue. Season, from July-September. Excellent as cut flower. Likes sunny position and prefers sandy soil. The glaucous blue foliage of this plant adds unusual colour to the border. My favourite, Oliverianum, a lovely blue.

FUNKIA (syn. Hosta). The Plantain Lily. A dwarf growing broad-leaved plant often grown entirely for its ornamental foliage. Bears white or lilac flowers in July on stems 1½-3 ft high. A plant that loves shade and moisture. Does well at the foot of a wall. My favourite, F. sieboldiana, a lilac white, 18 in. tall.

GAILLARDIA. An untidy grower which has few leaves. Flowers yellow and red of a daisy type. Height 2-3 ft and the flowering season from June-September. Easy to grow almost anywhere. My favourite, Ipswich Beauty, crimson with a golden edge, 3 ft tall.

GALEGA. Goat's Rue. Tall, feathery vetch-like plant, which bears white or mauve flowers in June or July. Grows 3-5 ft tall according to variety. Should be planted towards the back of the border to allow later flowers to conceal it after flowering. Does well almost anywhere. My favourite, Duchess of Bedford, a bright mauve, 3 ft tall.

GERANIUM PRATENSE. Commonly called Cranesbill. (Should not be confused with the bedding type of geranium, which is commonly given this name by amateurs.) This is a plant of neat bushy growth with attractive foliage. The leaves produce pretty autumn tints later. Grows 1-3 ft high, bearing blue, purple or crimson or pink flowers from June-July. Is good for the front of the border; likes light well drained soil. My favourite, Mrs. Kendall Clarke, because of its deep blue flowers on stems 1½ ft tall.

GEUM. A neat plant, with dwarf fern-like foliage. The strawberry-like flowers being borne on stems 1-3 ft tall. They may be yellow, orange or scarlet. It is often in season from June-September. Grand for the front of a border, loves a sunny position. My favourite, Dolly North, an orange double.

GYPSOPHILA. The most feathery plant for the border. Resembles a cloud of snow. Plants are covered with mounds of minute innumerable white flowers. Grows 3 ft high. Colour, white; though there is a pink, known as Rosy Veil. It is in season during July and August. Loves a chalky soil.

Prefers full sun. Resents disturbance. My favourite, Bristol Fairy, a strong white double.

HELENIUM. One of the best perennials for the autumn. Produces quantities of single daisy-like flowers with a coloured ball-like centre to them. Flowers vary in colour through yellows, coppers, crimson and bronzes, and the stems may be anything from 2-5 ft tall. The flowering season is normally September and October, but there are some July flowering types in the dwarf form. They suffer from lack of moisture in a dry season. Where shoots are crowded weak growth should be removed in spring. My favourite, Crimson Beauty, a bronzy red, 2 ft.

Helenium

HELIANTHUS. A Sunflower-like plant growing 5-8 ft tall. In season during August and September. Excellent for the back of the border. My favourite ,Morning Sun, the best double sunflower, with a profusion of rich orange-yellow flowers on stems $4\frac{1}{2}$ ft.

HEMEROCALLIS. The Day-lily. Has strap-like green foliage, with lily-like flowers freely produced during July and August. Each flower only lasts a day, and is followed by another produced higher up the stem. Grows 2-4 ft high. My favourite, Black Magic, ruby mahogany.

HEUCHERA. A dainty plant which resembles the common London Pride. The foliage is dwarf and compact; the flowers are dainty, minute and bell-like, being carried on slender stems $1\frac{1}{2}$-2 ft high. They may be red or pink in colour. Season June-July. My favourite, Pluie de feu, a cherry red. Must be grown in a warm well-drained spot.

INCARVILLEA. Provides a vivid splash of colour for the front of the border in early summer. Bears a trumpet-shaped flower and has handsomely toothed leaves. Likes full sun and a deep, sandy soil. Height $1\frac{1}{2}$ ft. Season June-July. My favourite, I. delavayi, a deep rose.

IRIS. See Chapter 14, specialist Flower Borders.

KNIPHOFIA. Red-hot pokers. Their English name describes them well. They have long narrow spreading leaves and long spikes of flowers which when in bloom resemble torches or pokers. The height is 3-5 ft and the colour yellow, orange to scarlet. They flower from June to October according to variety. They love deep rich soil, and in dry weather they must be watered freely. My favourite, Earliest of All, an intense scarlet.

LINUM. The Flax. This is both the linen and the linseed

plant. The flowers may be blue or yellow; the plants are dainty, the stems are from 1-1½ ft tall and the season from May to July. The plants are grand for the front of a border. My favourite variety, narbonense, a lovely sky-blue 18 in. tall.

LOBELIA. Not the ordinary little blue lobelia that people plant around the beds but Lobelia cardinalis. This plant bears brilliant crimson red flowers on tall spikes, 3 ft high. The season is July-September and the foliage is slightly reddish. The lobelia likes a moist rich soil and full sun. It is dangerous to leave it out during the winter as it is often killed by frost. My favourite, Queen Victoria, a vivid scarlet.

LUPINS. Grow 3-4 ft high and flower in June. They are gross feeders and must be planted where the soil does not dry out. They quickly exhaust themselves and it is always wise therefore to have a young stock of plants coming on. Never allow the seed heads to develop. There are a very large number of varieties with flowers in almost every colour and shade. My favourite, the Russell Lupins, which can be had in almost any colour desired.

LYCHNIS. The Campion. Most suited for the front of the border. Likes full sun. Grows 18 in. to 3 ft high and is in flower from June till August, the blossoms being pink and red shades. My favourite, L. chalcedonica, a brilliant scarlet, 3 ft.

LYTHRUM. A plant that makes nicely balanced bushes of olive green foliage, plus erect stems, with terminal spikes of rosy crimson flowers. Height 3-4 ft. Flowers from July till September. Quite likes semi-shade. Moisture lover, so give water freely in a dry summer. My favourite, Robert, a pink, 2 ft high.

MECONOPSIS. The blue poppy. Grows 1-4 ft high according to variety and flowers from June till August. There is a yellow type known as the Welsh poppy. Prefers to be planted in woodland drifts. Loves rich soil in leaf mould. My favourite M. Baileyi, which bears sky-blue pendant flowers on stems 4 ft high.

MICHAELMAS DAISY. See Aster Border.

MONARDA. Sometimes called the Eau de Cologne plant. Has lovely scented leaves and brilliant round cushion-like flowers which have trumpet petals around the edge. Through the middle of one flower another will grow. In season from July-October and grows 3 ft high. My favourite, Cambridge Scarlet.

MONTBRETIA. See Chapter 8.

NEPETA. Catmint. A compact dwarf grey leafed plant which bears masses of lavender-like flowers, from early summer until autumn. At its best in July. Grand for edging a border. Cats love to sit in it, and should be kept off as they may ruin it. Hates a badly drained wet soil. My favourite, Six Hills Giant, 3 times larger than the normal type.

ŒNOTHERA. The Evening Primrose. Makes a lovely golden yellow display throughout the summer. The flowers open towards the evening and die the next day but they are produced in profusion and so the plant always looks well. Prefers a light soil. Height 6 in. to 5 ft. Colour bright yellow. My favourite, Yellow River, seems always in bloom. Quite likes a damp spot.

PÆONY. One of the most gorgeous of all border plants. Has strikingly ornamental foliage and large ball-like blooms diffusing perfume. Height 3 ft, flowers May to the end of July. May be had as a white, cream, pink or red. There are three main divisions – the double and single Chinese, the May flowering and the Imperial group. My favourite 'Chinese' is Lady Alexandra Duff, my favourite May flowerer, Mme Calot, and my favourite satiny pink Claire Dubois, a rose and gold. Flowers in late June and early July. Pæonies look well when planted in groups alone. They are gross feeders and hate being moved.

PAPAVER. The Oriental Poppy. Wonderfully effective when grouped. Give a kind of oriental splendour to a border. Grows $2\frac{1}{4}$-4 ft high and in flower from May-early June. Flowers may be crimson, salmon, scarlet, pink or white. Extremely untidy growers and unless well staked, flop badly. After flowering they look very untidy and bare. Try and grow gypsophila in front of them. Like a sunny position. My favourite variety Goliath, almost an exact replica of a very large Flanders poppy.

PHLOX. One of the most popular flowers. Grows 2-4 ft high and it can be in flower from July to September. The large heads of flowers may be white, pink, mauve or purple. Excellent in borders for early August when there is little else about. Have large clumps in the centre rows. Loves full sun. Thin out growths which come up in the spring.

My favourite varieties, Skylight, the bluest of all, Firefly, rose with deeper centre, and Endurance, a shaded salmon.

PHYSOSTEGIA. Also known as *DRACOCEPHALUM.* I am putting this in because it is such a fine plant for the late summer border. It bears stout stems and its flower spikes resemble those of the heath. It grows 1½ ft high, it is crimson in colour and is at its best in September. My favourite, P. Vivid.

POLYGONATUM. Commonly called Solomon's Seal. It produces arching fronds and green foliage from the undersides of whoch hang small white bells in clusters. It loves shade, grows to a height of 2-3 ft and is in season during June and July.

POTENTILLA. Nice in the front of a border because of its brilliant colour. Likes full sun. Grows to a height of 2 ft and flowers from June till August. May be had as orange, pink, yellow and red. My favourite, Fire Dance, an orange salmon and scarlet, 12 in.

PULMONARIA. Sometimes given the awful name of Lung Wort. Excellent for the early spring as it flowers in May. Often has variegated leaves, bearing blue or red and sometimes blue and red, flowers on stems 6 in. high. Will put up with partial shade.

PYRETHRUM. One of the best herbaceous flowers. Grows to a height of 2-3 ft, bearing daisy-like blooms, pink, red, white single or double. The foliage is feathery and fern-like and the season is June. My favourite, Margery Robinson, a single bright pink. Loves plenty of organic matter. Dislikes drought.

RUDBECKIA. A useful autumn flowering plant but if allowed to spread too much may become a nuisance. Will grow 2-7 ft high according to variety. The flowers may be yellow, bronze or crimson and the season September and October. My favourite, R. speciosa, a rich yellow with a black cone, 3 ft. It loves moisture and does best on heavy soil.

udbeckia

SALVIA. A bushy type of plant with long flower spikes covered with little blooms. Height 3-4 ft, season July-September. Flowers blue or purple. They do best in full sun and will put up with quite hot dry soil. Love a mulching of organic matter in March. My favourite, S. virgata nemorosa (syn. Superba), 3 ft, flowers July.

SCABIOSA. The perennial scabious. A lovely flower of

pin cushion type which must grow in well drained soil — loves lime and full sun. Hates disturbance. Flowers are blue, mauve or white, on stems 2½ ft high, and in season from July-October. My favourite, Clive Greaves, a deep mauve.

SIDALCEA. Worth while including because of its lovely pink or reddish flower spikes. Quite an unusual type. In season in July and August. Grows to a height of 3-4 ft depending on the variety. There are mauves and whites but most of the good varieties are pink. My favourite, Rose Queen, a rose-pink 4 ft. Always plant in bold groups.

SOLIDAGO. The Golden Rod. Apt to spread tremendously and therefore to become too common. May be had in varieties that grow from 1 to 6 ft. Flowers of arching sprays are always yellow. Season August-Steptember, continuing sometimes till well on in October. My favourite S. Goldenmosa, has more solid heads than most varieties. Grows 3 ft high.

SPIRÆA. Commonly called Meadow Sweet. Has lovely ornamental foliage and feathery plumes of flowers. May grow from 2-6 ft. Colour white, pink or red. In season July till August. Loves a damp situation, and revels in rich soil. My favourite S. bullata, a rose red, 3 ft high.

STATICE (syn. Limonium). The Sea Lavender. Bears mauve or violet flowers, gracefully with cloud like sprays. Good for the front of the border. May be cut, dried, and used for winter decoration. My favourite, Violetta, a violet blue, 2½ ft.

THALICTRUM. The Meadow Rue. Very dainty foliage, lovely unusual flowers. Grows well in almost any soil. Hates shallow planting. Colours purple or yellow. In season in July and August. Height 3-6 ft. My favourite, Hewitt's double, a violet, 5 ft.

THERMOPSIS. A lupin-like plant but of stiffer growth. Grows 2 ft high, is yellow in colour. Its season is June and July. Likes a light chalky soil.

TRADESCANTIA. An unusual mauvy-blue flowered plant 1½ ft in height. Its reed-like leaves remain tidy throughout the summer. A grand plant for the town garden. Quite likes semi-shade, flowers in July. My favourite, Isis, an Oxford blue.

TROLLIUS. Rather like a huge double buttercup. Loves dampish soil, and in dry summers must be watered copiously. Colours yellow and orange, height 18 in. to 3 ft. My favourite, Fireglobe, a deep orange, 2½ ft tall. Flowers May-June.

VERBASCUM. Bears tall stately spikes of flowers from large leaves formed in rosettes. Height 4-6 ft. Colour yellow and bronze. Season June and July. Should be planted in the back of the border. Likes sun. My favourite, Cotswold Queen, a 4 ft buff terra-cotta.

VERONICA. Bears short spikes of flowers which last a short period only. In season in July. Height 1-3 ft. Colour always blue. My favourite, Shirley Blue, which grows 12 in. high only.

6 Annual Flowers and the Annual Border

There is no cheaper way of having a lovely flower border than by sowing annuals, for an annual is a plant that grows from seed, flowers, produces more seed and dies within twelve months. Normally annuals are sown in the spring to flower in the summer, but there are some hardy annuals that can be sown in August or September and live through the winter to flower earlier in the spring in consequence.

Position. All annuals like an open sunny position and prefer a nice South border and good soil but not specially rich soil. Some, like nasturtiums, prefer poor soil. Nasturtiums, if they grow in rich land, make a mass of leaves and few flowers.

Soil Preparation. See that the strip of ground in which the annuals are to be sown is so cultivated that all perennial weeds are eliminated. The land should be shallowly dug or forked in the autumn so as to allow the surface of the ground to become pulverized by the frost and winds. During the forking sedge peat can be added at the rate of a bucketful to the sq. yard. It will be easy to get the surface down to a fine state of tilth, as it is called, in which the small seeds will grow well.

Give a second light forking at least a fortnight before seed sowing, to allow the land to settle. It is a bad thing to sow small seeds on what is called a hollow seed bed. Tread the ground firmly before sowing or the baby seeds may be lost in air crevices. Should the ground be sticky it is useless to attempt to prepare it until it has dried somewhat. A seed bed should be moist but never gluey.

Lime and Liming. The ground must not be acid and so normal dressings of lime should be given. An annual border might receive hydrated lime every fourth year in January .at 3-4 oz to the sq. yard. Some annuals, scabious for instance, like a light sprinkling of lime each year on the strip of land where they are to grow.

Seed Sowing. For the annual flower border the seed should be sown in drifts in a similar way that planting is done in the case of the herbaceous border. Having prepared the ground and raked it level and seen that it is firm, it is possible then to scratch with a pointed stick, drifts of varying shapes into which the seeds of the various kinds of annuals are to be sown. These odd-shaped 'patches' should have the annual seed sown *very* thinly in them. Naturally the shorter plants will be sown towards the front of the border, the moderately growing ones about the middle of the border and the taller ones at the back.

As each kind of seed is sown in its particular little drift, the patch should be labelled clearly. Some people take the trouble to make a plan of their border first of all on squared paper and having drawn the drifts on this in pencil and labelled each one carefully, they then transfer their paper plan on to the actual strip of land concerned.

Having sown the seeds very thinly, rake the ground over lightly just to cover them. In very dry weather it may be worth while giving a good watering a day or two later through the fine rose of a can, but if the soil has been properly prepared and damped peat incorporated this overhead irrigation should not really be necessary. Those who feel they cannot sow thinly enough should mix the seed with dry sand. You need about 4 times the amount of sand to seed. If you want to see the seed as it falls on to the ground it is a good plan to whiten it well with lime before sowing.

Thinning. Any seed may be tiny and an annual flower seed usually is. It may produce a very tall plant. The Larkspur is an example. The seed is about the size of a pin's head and yet I have known the plants to grow to 6 ft high and be 3 ft or so across. Naturally, all annuals do not grow as high. I merely mention the fact to show the need for thinning the plants out as soon as they come through, for however much I stress thin sowing, people never do it sufficiently well. So thin to give the plants plenty of room for development. A plant that grows 9 in. high will want about 9 in. of room. Give it $4\frac{1}{2}$ in. on either side.

Some people take the trouble to thin three or four times. They thin out first of all, say, one inch apart and then to two inches apart and so on. By doing this they are able to transplant the baby thinnings to any blank spots in the border that may appear. In this way gapping up can be done successfully. The annuals sown in late August or mid September are often not thinned out till the following February or March. They are allowed to grow on through the winter somewhat thickly with the idea that one plant protects another. During thinning a certain amount of hand weeding can be done and it is necessary to be able to recognize weed seedlings from annuals.

Those who are growing annuals for the first time would do well to sow a few seeds of each kind they are going to grow in a box, placed in the greenhouse or even in a warm room near the light. See that the soil in the box is watered regularly and that the rows of annuals are labelled. As a result the plants in the box will be up and recognizable some three weeks or so before those growing out-of-doors, and the beginner with have no difficulty in recognizing each variety when thinning.

Cultivations. In an annual border of this type with drifts of one kind of annual growing, as it were, into another, it is very difficult to use the hoe at all. With care it is possible to do a certain amount of stirring between plants by using a Dutch hoe almost perpendicularly and just cutting through the top half inch of soil in order to kill weed seeds just as they are germinating. This work has of course to be done in and around the annuals after they have been thinned.

To prevent weeds from growing, garden owners should cover the bed with powdery brown home-made compost an inch deep all over the bed and in between and among the sown annuals. Those who have not made their own compost will use medium grade sedge peat instead. This organic mulching will prevent the annual weeds from growing and thus no hoeing will be necessary.

Staking. Annuals grow very quickly and in consequence need staking early. They do not have quite the same resistance as perennials and thus they are easily damaged by wind or heavy rain. The ideal method of support is by the use of pea sticks pushed in and among the plants. The smaller the plant, the shorter the twiggy stick used. The annuals grow up in and among the twiggy supports provided. They hide the sticks and yet grow naturally. The only annuals that are grown up bamboos, as a rule, are sweet peas which are often provided with individual 8 ft canes.

In the annual border they grow satisfactorily up a group of hazel or beech sticks and make a nice clump in consequence.

Dead Flower Removal. Keep removing the dead flower heads. Never allow the annuals to go to seed. You will thus prolong the flowering period of the great majority of annuals, and in addition, the plants will have a much tidier appearance.

Watering and Mulching. If waterings have to be done in a dry summer do not give light sprinklings but soak the ground thoroughly either in the evening or early in the morning. Use one of those whirling sprinklers attached to a hose for the purpose, and leave the sprinkler in position for half an hour. Then move it for the next half hour to another part of the border so that a good quantity of artificial rain is given. Apply damp sedge peat in among the plants to a depth of one inch in the summer to help conserve the moisture in the ground.

GOING ON HOLIDAY. If you are going on holiday for a fortnight or so and the annual border is in full flower, it is worth while cutting back all the plants fairly severely to prevent seeding taking place which you are away. Then when you return, the border should be in full bloom again.

Cut Flower Borders

Annuals make excellent cut flowers and special borders in a 'reserve' part of the garden may be used for the purpose. The annuals are sown in rows 1 ft apart, the drills being half an inch deep. The seeds are sown thinly and thinning out is done as advised for annuals in the general border. Support may be given to the plants by pushing a bamboo into the end of each row and then by stretching string in such a way that it surrounds the plants from end to end. Two strings are usually used, one to go round the plants on one side, and one on the other side.

The flowers should be cut when about half developed, with as long a stem as possible. They should be gathered early in the morning or late in the evening, and placed immediately into deep receptacles containing water, being put in 'up to their necks.' If left like this for two or three hours they gorge themselves with moisture and thus last longer in the vases in consequence.

For cut flowers annuals are often sown in the autumn because naturally they are more valuable when produced early in the season. Those who live in the north can ensure that the annuals live through if they cover the rows with continuous cloches, and even those with southern gardens will find that they can have their cut flower annuals three weeks or so earlier if they cover with these simple 'miniature greenhouses' in January.

Annuals which have proved to be good cut flowers and which can be sown in the autumn are cornflower, candytuft, larkspur, calendula, and love in the mist. Other good cut flower annuals which are generally sown in the spring without cloche coverage are clarkia, godetia, annual gypsophila, the annual chrysanthemum, saponaria, and sweet sultan.

Half-hardy Annuals

In this chapter we have been discussing the hardy annuals – those that can be sown out of doors in the autumn or early in the spring. There are a number of annuals known as half-hardy, which have been sown in a greenhouse, frame or under access frames and must be allowed to grow there until such time as the weather is warm enough either to plant them out of doors, or in the case of cloches or frames to allow them to be removed. It is possible to make open-air sowings, with half-hardy annuals late, say, about the middle of May, but as a result the flowers are late also.

Greenhouse Sowing. Most sowings are made in February or March in the greenhouse at a temperature of 55-60 degrees Fahrenheit. A sedge-peat and sand no-soil compost is bought and filled into boxes, pots or pans which have been thoroughly cleaned beforehand. They should be well crocked and provided with good drainage holes. The no-soil compost in the boxes is then firmed and made level and the seeds sown over the top thinly. The smaller seeds should be covered by sifting a little fine silver sand over the top. Water the boxes or pots through the fine rose of a can and stand them on the staging of the greenhouse, shaded for the first few days with a sheet of paper.

Thin the seedlings out when large enough to handle and if necessary prick some of the seedlings out into further boxes. Give the plants a hardening off process (a) by gradually supplying more ventilation in the house, and (b) by taking the plants out afterwards into a frame before they are planted out into the open.

Be very careful of the damping-off disease when the seedlings are in their young stage. This can be prevented by (1) sowing thinly, (2) thinning early, (3) preventing the atmosphere of the house from becoming damp and stuffy, (4) by not watering overhead but by immersing the box or pot in a bath of water for a minute or two and (5) by watering with a 'cure' known as Cheshunt Compound.

Frame Sowing. Those who have no greenhouse may sow the seed thinly in frames, either in the soil direct or into boxes or pans stood in frames. It is convenient to sterilize the soil used and thus there is no weed competition nor trouble from diseases or pests.

Cloche or Access Frame Sowings. In this case the cloches are put into position over the ground a fortnight before seed sowing is to be done in order to warm the strip of land concerned. The seed is then sown in very shallow drills and the plants thinned out as soon as the seedlings are fit to handle. It is useful to prepare the soil before sowing and make it as near as possible to the compost used for the boxes by adding sedge peat and sand. The ends of the cloche rows are closed with sheets of glass to keep out draughts. The plants harden off automatically under cloches and when the middle of May comes and there is no further fear of frost (at any rate in the south) the cloches may be removed.

Cut Flower Half-hardys. There are a few half-hardy annuals that are especially useful as cut flowers. China Asters, for instance, which normally flower in July and August; ten-week stocks which flower at the same time, East Lothian stocks, which from August sowings will flower from May to the end of August and from February sowings begin to flower in June; zinnias which can be cut in August and September, and cosmos which comes into use during these two months also.

The China Aster is usually sown at the end of March as are the ten-week stocks. The East Lothian stock seed is sown in July or August; the zinnias should be sown at the end of March and the cosmos about the middle of March.

Everlasting Annuals

There are a number of everlasting flowers that can be grown as hardy annuals, though none of them succeeds from autumn sowings out of doors. The three most popular are :

HELICHRYSUM. Can be had in white, yellow, pink, crimson and bronze; it grows to a height of 2 ft as a rule, and flowers from July to September. The plants need to be thinned out to 9 in. apart. In the south it is possible to sow this annual at the beginning of October under cloches.

RHODANTHE. Is a very pleasing little plant similar in habit and growth to Helichrysum but smaller – never more than 1 ft tall, and the colour of the flowers is either pink or white. When sown out of doors early in April it blooms in June and July. It needs about 6 in. of room only.

Helichrysum

STATICE. The Sea Lavender, can be had in white, yellow, blue and mauve. It grows about 15 in. high, and is in flower in July, August and September according to variety. The seed may be sown under glass in February or early in March, the plants being put out of doors during May. The most popular types are S. sinuata, which can be had in blue, white or rose; S. sinuata suworowi has a shorter flowering period and sells well in June. It is usually sown under glass in March and planted out late in April or early in May, and S. latifolia which grows 2 ft high and is usually planted in well-drained soil in March or April. It is generally propagated by lifting and dividing old plants in the spring. The statice or sea lavender seems to like light soil, well drained, and has no objection to slight applications of salt.

ACROLINIUM. Properly called Helipterum from the words Helios and pteron, a feather. Among the most graceful of the everlasting annuals; seeds are often sown under glass in March and the seedlings transplanted early in May. The acrolinium grows to a height of about $1\frac{1}{2}$ ft and bears single rose-pink flowers about $1\frac{1}{2}$ in. in diameter. The flowers close up in dull weather but the double varieties are less inclined to do so and in consequence are generally more decorative. There is a white form also. There is a new strain of double flowered varieties, of many pleasing shades, bearing from carmine-rose to creamy yellow flowers. The seed is usually sold under the name of Acrolinium grandiflorum.

GOMPHRENA. Bears attractive bell-shaped flowers on stems about 18 in. high. Seeds are usually sown under cloches or in frames in March and the seedlings transplanted towards the end of April. There are various coloured forms including whites, pinks and purples. May be sown out of doors about the end of April in the usual way.

XERANTHEMUM. Grows about 2 ft high and bears numerous purple tapering everlasting flowers about 2 in. in diameter. Can be had as a full double rose colour, a double purple, a double white, as well as a semi-double purple and semi-double white.

WAITZIA. A very unusual everlasting which is now seldom grown. It is a half-hardy, the flowers being borne in terminal clusters. Seeds are usually sown under glass early in April, the seedlings being transplanted into a sunny position early in June. The flowers are usually borne on stems 18 in. to 2 ft high. There are yellows, whites and pinks.

List of Annuals with Brief Descriptions

It is impossible in a book of this size to list all the annuals that are available and I have chosen quite arbitrarily the annuals I have found to be (a) easy to grow, (b) full of colour, (c) last over a long period. Annuals of varying heights, shades and types have been chosen.

ADONIS. Looks something like a buttercup, but has very pretty finely cut foliage. The seed may be sown in the open ground at the beginning of April. A. æstivalis grows 18 in. high and bears deep crimson flowers in June and July. A. autumnalis grows 1 ft high bearing crimson flowers with a deeper centre from June to September.

AGERATUM. A half-hardy annual excellent for bedding work. The seed is sown in the greenhouse in February or March and the plants raised put into the open in May. Blue Ball is a handsome dwarf type with deep blue flowers carried in ball-shaped clusters. Blue Chip is a small flowered compact variety, splendid for edging.

ALYSSUM. An excellent bedding plant bearing deliciously scented white flowers. The seed can be sown in the open ground during April. Carpet of Snow makes a dwarf bushy plant about 3 in. high. Royal Carpet as its name suggests is a rich deep violet purple.

AMARANTHUS. Commonly known as Love-lies-Bleeding, grows to a height of 2-3 ft, the leaves being pale green and the flowers hanging in long drooping 'cords'. These strange flowers are a rich blood red. The seed is usually sown in the open ground in April.

There are other types of Amaranthus, like the Flaming Fountain; the leaves of this are flame coloured and the flower spikes are dark red.

ARCTOTIS. Generally treated as a half-hardy annual. Most varieties bear dazzling daisy-like flowers. A. grandis grows 1½ ft in height. The flowers have glistening white petals with the reverse shaded a delicate lavender. The grows 1½ ft in height. The flowers have glistening white flower centres are a rich blue. A. grandis only grows 2 ft high and has bright orange flowers on short stalks.

ASPERULA. The Woodruff. A nice little edging plant. Sow in the open in April. Usually flowers in June and July.

A. orientalis bears sky blue flowers on stems 1 ft high. Blossoms are sweetly scented.

BRACHYCOME. A dainty half-hardy that likes a dry sunny position. Flowers over a long period. Raise under glass in early April, transplant in the open towards the end of May. Can also be sown in open ground towards the beginning of May. B. iberidifolia grows 1 ft in height, flowers may be $1\frac{1}{2}$ in. in diameter in numerous varieties.

CALENDULA. Commonly called the Marigold, or the Pot Marigold. May be grown almost anywhere and proves an excellent cut flower. Sow in open ground from late March to May according to the weather and district. In the south, September sowings are often successful. May grow to a height of 2 ft and bear lovely orange-coloured or yellow flowers. Orange King is one of the best orange doubles, compact and free flowering. Radio has quilled and pointed rich orange petals. Orange Coronet has double golden orange and Geisha Girl double orange incurving petals.

CAMPANULA. Usually thought of as a perennial or biennial but there are some annuals that can be sown indoors in March and the plants raised then put out in the middle of May. C. compatica Blue Clips is a pretty species with blue flowers – cup-like. Looks well as a pot plant in a greenhouse. C. persicifolia only grows 2 ft high.

CHINA ASTER. Seed usually sown in the greenhouse in March or in a cold frame in April. Seedlings are transplanted into further boxes or frames 2-3 in. apart and when danger of frost is past the plants are put out into the open about the end of May. Is very subject to a disease known as Black Leg, causing the stems to rot off at ground level. Where it is known to occur the soil should always be sterilized before the seed is sown. There are many types and strains. The Anemone-flowered which are very handsome for indoor decoration, are mid-season, with stems often 2 ft long. There are the Colour Carpet Mixed, the dwarfs that only grow 9 in. high. There are the Giants of California, the large flowered types, 2 ft in height – the latest of all; Giant Comets which are excellent for bedding and cutting; Bouquet Powder Puffs, 2 ft, medium sized, rounded, unusual. Lilliput is also mid-season but small flowered and very floriferous. Ostrich Feather is the long-stemmed type usually 2 ft in height and mid-season.

CHRYSANTHEMUM. The annual species of chrysanthemum are not sufficiently well known. Few annuals give a better show. Seeds are usually sown in open ground during April or under cloches may be made early in March. Good varieties are : Cecilia – a white with gold zones, very vigorous, height 2½ ft; Paludosum – a dwarf, bushy, free flowering – pure white flowers, height 1 ft; Gaiety – produces double flowers in a range of colours, height 2 ft.

CLARKIA. Easy to cultivate. Seed usually sown in open ground in March and April, or under continuous cloches early in March. May also be sown in September, out-of-doors and covered with continuous cloches early in November. C. pulchella has semi-double flowers with broad petals. Unwins Double Mixed is an unusual blending.

COBÆA. One of the climbing types. C. scandens is the only species usually cultivated. It is grand for climbing up rustic arches and fences. The flowers are 1½ in. in diameter resembling a Canterbury bell, being of a light violet colour. The seed is usually sown under glass early in March and the seedlings are transplanted early in June to a warm sunny position.

COREOPSIS. Usually thought of as a perennial but there are annual kinds which in seedsmen's catalogues are often sold as Calliopsis. Plants are usually raised from seed sown under cloches or in the greenhouse or frames during March, the seedlings being transplanted about the end of May into the open. It is quite possible however to sow out of doors in April, especially in the south. C. tinctoria grows about 2 ft high. There are the semi-dwarf varieties like Baby Sun, a single golden yellow, free flowering, 18 in.

COSMOS. Sometimes called Cosmea. Has delicately cut foliage and large single or double flowers. A grand annual. Seeds are usually sown under glass early in April, the seedlings being transplanted at the end of May or early in June. Can be sown in the open about the third week of April. There are a number of varieties including : Bright Lights, semi-double flowers orange, red – yellow, all early flowering – 2½ ft; Sunset, semi-double Vermilion red – 3 ft; Goldcurl, semi-double orange-yellow – 2 ft; Psyche, semi-double mixture of colours – very free flowering – 3 ft.

DELPHINIUM. See Larkspur.

DIANTHUS. The Annual Carnation, D. caryophyllus. It is the Chabaud varieties which are excellent for cutting if sown under Access Frames in February or early March or if sown in the greenhouse in February with the plants put out early in April. In the Giant Chabaud section there is Rose Queen, Purple King, Ruby Queen, Grenadin, a double scarlet. D. sinensis Persian Carpet Mixed is one of the most free-blooming of annuals. It only grows to about 9 in. high and the flowers vary in colour from pink to rosy lilac. There is Heddewigii which grows 9 in. high and bears large single flowers varying in colour from crimson to white. There is Heddewigii Dwarf Sensation Mixed and Heddewigii Festival Mixed, the double type.

In the Sweet Wivelsfield group which was obtained by crossing Sweet William with Dianthus you have a plant which grows to about 18 in. and resembles the Sweet William. Queen of Hearts, an F.I. Hybrid, grows 1 ft high, produces a bushy plant 12 in. across covered with scarlet flowers. Bravo grows 10 in. high, bears masses of scarlet flowers, almost continuously throughout the summer. It is usually treated as an annual and is sown under glass in March or early April.

The new dwarf Sweet William

DIMORPHOTHECA. A South African sun-loving daisy-flowered plant. The flowers close during the evening and in cloudy weather. There is the Namaqualand Daisy that grows about 18 in. high and produces numbers of rich golden glossy flowers. There are the Aurantiaca hybrids which include shades from yellow to salmon, to orange and white.

ESCHSCHOLTZIA. One of the most brilliant annuals to grow. New forms continue to make their appearance. Sow seeds in open ground in September, certainly in the south, and you will get very early flowers, or of course sow in March or early April out-of-doors. E. californica grows 1 ft tall and can be had as singles or doubles. I can recommend the Monarch Art Shades – semi-double and frilled in various colours.

FELICIA. A daisy flowered genus, useful for edgings. Seeds are usually sown under glass in March and the seedlings transplanted early in May. F. adfinis grows 8 in. high and is often used as a decorative pot plant. F. fragilis grows 6 in. high and bears clear blue flowers, being a first class edging plant.

GODETIA. A very bright annual. Seeds usually sown in open ground in September to flower the following summer,

Aquilegia 'McKanna Giants'

or in the north sow in spring. G. grandiflora grows 2 ft high. This is the best species of which the majority of garden varieties have been derived. I can recommend Cherry Red and Flesh Pink. Those who prefer varieties growing only 1 ft high may have Kelvedon Glory, Sybil Sherwood, a bright salmon pink, and Scarlet Emblem, a rich crimson. There are compact varieties growing only 9 in. high, for instance, Gorgeous, a blood red, and Monarch dwarf.

GYPSOPHILA. The Cloud Plant. A very graceful plant used for table decoration. Also giving featheriness and lightness to a border. Seed usually sown in open ground in early April, or for cut flower work under cloches in October. G. elegans grows 18 in. high, bearing dainty white flowers, while Elegans Rosea bears rosy pink flowers.

HELIANTHUS. The Sunflower. Seeds are usually sown in April in the ground where the plants are to flower. There is the common yellow sunflower that often grows 8 ft high.

Giant Sunflowers (Helianthus) provide an unusual background to a photograph.

It has varieties like Sutton's Red whose large yellow flowers have a broad chestnut band round the centre. There is the Miniature Sunflower called Dwarf Sungold, which is perhaps more decorative and bears numerous yellow flowers to a height of only 3-4 ft.

HELICHRYSUM. See Everlastings, page 59.

HELIPTERUM. See Everlastings, page 59.

ICELAND POPPY. See Papaver nudicaule.

IMPATIENS. The Balsam. Seed sown in open ground in April flower well in the summer. There is the garden balsam or Lady's Slipper, a tender annual which is sown under glass at a temperature of 70 degrees in March or early April, the seedlings not being transplanted till early June. There is the Camellia-flowered balsam, the large flowered double type that grows about 18 in. high. There is General Gursan, a red and white variegated, 5-9 in. high, the famous Zig-Zag Mixed with scarlet, orange, pink, rose and salmon flowers, and Holstii hybrids, a fine mixture of lovely colours.

IPOMÆA. A climbing annual with convolvulus-like flowers. The seeds are usually sown under glass in March or early April and the seedlings planted out in June. My favourites are the Early Call, a rose, the Flying Saucer, blue and white, and Wedding Bells, a soft mauve.

KOCHIA. Known as the Burning Bush. Grows to a height of 2-3 ft and makes a compact bush of pale green feathery foliage. In the autumn its leaves turn to a rich coppery red. Sow seeds under glass in April and plant out at the end of May.

LARKSPUR. Excellent cut flower. Can usually be sown out of doors late in September, the plants then reach to a height of 6 ft. If sown early in April in open ground plants usually grow 3-4 ft high and flower later than the autumn sowings. The Double Stock-flowered larkspurs are perhaps the best. They can be had in dark blue, azure blue, rosy scarlet, white and salmon rose. There are also the Dwarf Hyacinth Flowers with feathery foliage.

LATHYRUS. The Latin name for the Sweet Pea. Often grown by experts on the cordon system in specially prepared ground. Seeds can be sown under cloches in the open in October or in the greenhouse in January or for those who just want ordinary flowers, in the open ground in March or April. When grown on the cordon system only one stem is allowed and side shoots and the clingers or tendrils are pinched off. For the ordinary garden often grown up pea sticks are allowed to produce flowers at will. The important thing with sweet peas is never to allow the pods or seeds to form. There are a tremendous number of varieties, some of which I recommend on page 164.

LAVATERA. Grows to a height of 3 ft and bears rosy purple flowers. Seeds are usually sown in the open during April but in the south I have known seeds to be sown in a warm sheltered border in September, and plants resulting live through the winter. Of the varieties available I recommend Loveliness.

LINARIA. The Toadflax. An excellent little garden plant which may be raised from seed sown in the open during March and April. L. maroccana, the 1 ft handsome plant, bears dense violet flowers, with its various varieties and hybrids.

LINUM. Flax. A lovely annual, extremely free flowering. The seeds are usually sown in the open in April, where the plants are to flower. There are two types, L. grandiflorum, like Regale, which grows to a height of 3 ft and may bear flowers 2 in. in diameter. There is Little Snow White which bears small white flowers on stems 8 in. tall.

LOVE-IN-THE-MIST. See Nigella.

LOVE-LIES-BLEEDING. See Amaranthus.

LUPINUS. The Annual Lupin. Most people think of lupins as perennials and many of them are. The annual lupins however, are very effective and flourish in most soils. Seed should be sown in April in the open where the plants are to flower. Perhaps the most popular of the annual lupins is Hartwegii which grows to a height of 3 ft. L. Cruckshanksii grows 4 ft high and bears large fragrant rose and yellow flowers. A dwarf annual lupin is L. nanus, which is about 9 in. tall and very free flowering. The blossoms are blue and lilac.

MALLOW. There is only one annual species of any merit. Malva crispa. This is an upright grower, 5 ft high. The leaves are crisp and curled and the flowers are small and white. The foliage is sometimes used for garnishing purposes in the kitchen. Sow seed under glass (cloche, frame or greenhouse) late in March. Transplant the seedlings into the open early in June.

MALOPE. An old-fashioned annual that loves rich soil

and a sunny position. Sow the seeds in the open ground late in April. The most popular type is M. trifida which grows to a height of 3 ft. It bears large rosy-purple flowers in profusion; a variety grandiflora has larger flowers, rosy red and veined inside with deeper red.

MALVA. See Mallow.

MARIGOLD. See Calendula.

MATHIOLA. See Stock.

NASTURTIUM. See Tropæolum.

NEMESIA. Because of their wide range of brilliant colour and wealth of bloom these South African annuals are now very popular. Seed grown out of doors does germinate with difficulty but the best way to raise the plants is to sow seed in pots or boxes in a cold frame, or under cloches and not in the greenhouse or out of doors. Plant the seedlings in the open towards the end of May. The most popular species today is N. strumosa which grows to a height of 18 in. Some of the best varieties are Blue Gem, a brilliant blue, Fire King, a scarlet, Orange Prince, a rich deep orange, and Unwins hybrids which grow 10 in. high.

NEMOPHILA. Californian Bluebell. A lovely pretty compact annual bearing bright bell-shaped flowers. Sow the seeds where the plants are to bloom, in September, and they will give a wealth of flowers the following year, or sow them in April the following year. The best species is N. insignis, known as Baby Blue Eyes.

NICOTIANA. The Tobacco plant. Generally grown for the fragrance it gives off in the evening. The seed is usually sown under glass late in March and the seedlings put out towards the end of May. Can be sown in open border late in May and as a result it is late in flowering. N. affinis has within its 'family' Crimson Bedder, a deep crimson, and Idol, which is smaller. Lime Green grows to a height of 2 ft and has greeny yellow flowers.

NIGELLA. Love-in-the-Mist or Devil-in-the-Bush. One of the most popular flowers there is. Sow the seed towards the end of September out of doors for flowering early the following summer; covering with continuous cloches ensures flowering in May. May be sown out of doors in March and then flowers about July. N. damascena grows about 2 ft high and bears pale blue or white blossoms. Miss Jekyll is the most popular, cornflower blue. There is also the Persian Jewels with flowers of rose, pink, carmine, mauve, purple, etc.

PAPAVER. See Poppy.

PETUNIA. Generally grown as a bedding plant, the seeds being sown in the greenhouse during February or March, the seedlings being planted out in June. There are all double strains both tall and dwarf; there are striped and blotched strains like Hender's and there are the Double Grandifloras, a large-flowered strain in a great variety of colours. There are the bedding varieties that grow about 1 ft high and can be had under various names like Blue Ribbon, a blue, Orange Bells, an orange, Red Satin, a red, and Sugar Plum, an orchid lavender.

PHACELIA. The seeds are usually sown in open ground in late September for flowering next year, and in the cold parts of the north the seeds should be sown in April for flowering in the summer. P. campanularia only grows 9 in. high and bears brilliant blue flowers and greyish green leaves tinged with red. There are other species but this is the most important.

PHLOX. The annual phlox is Phlox drummondii which grows about 1½ ft high and is a very showy plant. Though it can be sown out of doors late in April it is usually sown under some form of glass in March and the plants are put out in late May or early June. There are a number of types such as Twinkle Dwarf Star, a mixture of colours; nana compacta Cecily Mixed; and Unwin's Large Flowered.

POLYGONUM. The annual in this genus are quite attractive. There is P. orientale, the Prince's Feather which often grows 5 ft high and bears crimson flowers in long drooping spirals. P. persicaria the Lady's Thumb grows 2 ft high, and there is the sign of the thumb in every leaf. The flowers vary from pink to purple.

POPPY. Papaver. A border of poppies is a constant joy for many weeks. Annual poppies are easy to grow. The seed can be sown in the open ground in March or April. In the case of P. nudicaule the seed should be sown at the end of July under continuous cloches or in a cold frame, and the seedlings that result should be planted in September where they are to flower next year. This Iceland Poppy group is undoubtedly very popular. The flowers may be had in almost any colour. The Gartref is a unique strain composed of petals edged with a deeper strain. The Sunbeam strain produces the largest of all the flowers. The corn poppy is P. rhœas. It has given rise to numerous garden varieties. Shirley Poppies which are very well known, while the Danneburg are the white cross on red types. I like also Pierrot, a bright scarlet single at 2 ft.

POT MARIGOLD. See Calendula.

RUDBECKIA. Sometimes called Black-eyed Susan. The seeds are usually sown in March under glass, the seedlings being planted out towards the end of May. Can of course be sown in the open towards the end of April. Does well started under continuous cloches if sown early in April. The annual is R. bicolor. It grows 1½ ft in height, the petals are generally yellow marked at the base with purple. The central disc is usually black. Bambi is a 1 ft rich chestnut and gold; Autumn Leaves, a 2 ft brown and bronze; and Sputnik, a lemon with a maroon centre.

SALPIGLOSSIS. The flowers are delicately marked and the trumpet-shaped blooms are particularly beautiful. Their colours may range from pale yellow to scarlet and from purple to blue. Seeds are usually sown under glass early in March so as to have plants ready to put out early in June. They make a wonderful show for weeks during the summer. Larger plants can be obtained by sowings made early in September under continuous cloches or in the greenhouse. Splash is earlier and more bushy than other strains with a wide colour range.

SAPONARIA. The seeds can be sown in open ground in September to flower the following summer except in the north when the seeds are usually sown in late April. Under cloches autumn sowings are even possible in the north. There are two main species : S. calabrica, 9 in. high, pink, of which there is a white and a scarlet variety, and S. vaccaria, the most graceful of the two, grows about 2½ ft tall and bears large deep pink flowers.

SCABIOSA. The Annual Scabious or Pin-cushion flower. Lovely flowers borne on long wiry stems. Sow in September under cloches, or sow early in March under cloches. Sowings made in the open towards the middle of April produce plants that flower late. S. atropurpurea grows 2 ft high. It is this species that produce most of the garden varieties. Blue Cockade is a dark blue and Fire King a rosy crimson. There are also the Cockade mixed seeds.

SHIRLEY POPPY. See Poppy.

STOCK (*Mathiola*). Stocks are so sweetly scented and flower for such long periods that most people want to grow them. It is possible to have a succession of blooms from early May till late autumn. M. bicornis is the night-scented stock. It is not much to look at in the day but the flowers open in the evening and give off a delicious perfume. Sow thinly where the plants are to grow, early in April. The Seven Week stocks produce one long densely flowered spike followed later by numerous side branches. This makes an excellent cut flower and may be had in a variety of colours. The Giant Perfection Ten Week large-flowering is an excellent stock as it grows to a height of 2 ft. The Ten Week Large Flowering is useful both for cutting and bedding. The Double Early Cascade stock is the shorter early flowering form and bears massive spikes of lilac flowers.

All the types mentioned above may be grown from seed, sowing in March in the greenhouse or under cloches and the seedlings transplanted where they are to flower about mid-May.

A number of stocks can be sown in the summer and autumn; the Brompton stock, for instance, is really a biennial. The seed is usually sown at the end of July and the seedlings put out where they are to flower in September.

SUNFLOWER. See Helianthus.

SWEET PEA. See Lathyrus.

SWEET SULTAN. See Centaurea, page 45.

TAGETES. The Marigold. Generally grown as a bedding plant, the seeds being sown in the greenhouse late in February or early in March and pricked out into further boxes, and planted out into the open in early May. There is the African marigold which has many varieties, like Sunbeam, a pale gold variety. Guinea Gold, a semi-double golden orange, and Mexican Harvest Gold, an all-double golden yellow. In the French Marigold group the modern plants only grow about 6 in. high. Red Carpet, a mahogany red. Golden Gem, a double golden yellow, and Carina a deep orange and Lemon Gem, a bright yellow.

TOBACCO PLANT. See Nicotiana.

TOUCH ME NOT. See Impatiens.

TROPÆOLUM. The Nasturtium. This thrives on poor soil for if grown on rich land you get nothing but leaves and few flowers. T. majus is the annual with varieties like Rose, a cerise rose, Salmon Baby, and Cherry Talisman, a scarlet. There are the Tom Thumb Globe varieties which produce small plants covered with flowers like Jewel Mixed.

URSINIA. A lovely South African annual with very graceful foliage and an abundance of orange daisy-like flowers. Being a half-hardy is it best to sow the seed under glass (greenhouse cloche or frame) in March or early April, the plants that arise being put out towards the end of May. It is possible to sow seed in open ground early in May. Ursinias like a sunny dryish position. U. anethoides grows to a height of 1½ ft and bears large rich orange flowers, 3 in. across on stiff, wiry stems. There is a deep red zone near the base of the petals marked with a showy black blotch.

VENIDIUM. Another South African annual with daisy-like flowers which are strikingly handsome. The seeds should be sown as advised for Ursinia above. It prefers poor soil and in fact in rich ground produces imperfectly-shaped flowers. V. fastuosum grows to a height of 2½ ft. The leaves are covered with white downy hairs and the flowers may be 5 in. across. The petals are deep orange and the centre of the flowers jet black. There are some hybrids which include several shades – orange, buff, yellow and white.

VERBENA. This is really a perennial treated as an annual. The seeds are sown in the greenhouse in January or early February in the no-soil compost and the seedlings are planted out towards the end of May or early June. Blaze is the one commonly grown and there is Sparkle Mixed which grows 10 in. high and produces large flowers of different colours, and Royal Banquet, which is really a mixture of many fine shades.

ZINNIA. A lovely tall brilliant annual excellent for cutting purposes but rather stiff and formal for border work. Seeds may be sown where the plants are to flower under continuous cloches towards the end of March or in greenhouses about the same time. After the usual potting on, the greenhouse plants are put out into their flowering positions in June. Zinnias like well manured ground, and a sunny spot. The Thumbelinas are little plants 6 in. high. Pumilas are 15 in. tall, bushy and bear 2½ in. diameter flowers. The Dahlia Flowered produce blooms like double dahlias 3-4 in. across. The Cactus Flowered grow 2½ ft high with a charming coloured range within them. The Peter Pans are dwarf bushy and bear incredibly large double flowers – and they bloom when they are only 6 in. high. Try Pan Pink, a salmon-rose.

How difficult it is to make a hard-and-fast rule dividing the annuals from the biennials! In the previous chapter I have already advised you to sow some annuals in the autumn and these of course live through the winter and bloom the following summer like biennials. Then there are some of the true biennials like the Evening Primrose for instance, which shed their seeds in the autumn and these will lie in the soil until early the following year before germinating. They thus grow and flower in one season and so seem like an annual. Then there is a number of perennials like the wallflower or sweet william which are always grown as biennials because they do better that way.

I have been purposely dictatorial in my choice of plants to be included in this chapter. The plants that are normally grown as biennials are mentioned.

The biennials will be raised in a seed bed very much in the same way as cabbages for planting out later, may be transplanted if necessary into further beds, and will finally be planted out into the place where they are going to grow.

Preparation of Seed Bed

As the seed of biennials are sown during the dry months of May, June and July, it is necessary to fork into the top 2 in. sedge peat at the rate of one bucketful to the sq. yard. If the soil is sandy and dry, damp the peat thoroughly beforehand. If it is heavy and tends to be wet, use the peat dry. In addition, work into the ground 'meat and bone' meal at 3 oz to the sq. yard. Make the bed really firm by treading, and follow this by a light raking, so as to get the surface down to a fine tilth (getting all the particles of soil down to a size smaller than a grain of wheat). The drills can then be drawn out shallowly, the right distance apart.

The Preparation of a 'Flowering' Bed

Here the land should be dug shallowly. Proper composted vegetable refuse should be incorporated shallowly at the rate of one bucketful to the sq. yard. This work should be done early so as to allow frosts and cold winds to act on any clods there may be and break them down. This, of course, can only be done if plants are to be set out in the spring. When planting is to be carried out in the autumn, the shallow digging and composting must be followed by a good treading to get the ground firm and ready for setting the plants out.

The compromise is to thin out the plants in the seed bed and to transplant them to a nursery bed. Here they may go on growing until they are finally planted into their flowering quarters in the spring. The nursery bed should be well enriched with fine organic matter like sedge peat, so that an abundance of fibrous roots may be produced.

Seed Sowing

Having prepared the seed bed, the drills will be drawn out 6 or 9 in. apart, and about half an inch deep, and the seeds of the biennials will be sown in these drills very thinly. To enable the beginner to do this, it is a good plan to mix the seed with five times the quantity by bulk of sand or pulverized dry earth. Some will prefer to sow the seed by stations, and in this case they will place 2 or 3 seeds every 6 in. along the drills, later thinning down to one seedling per station, should the germination prove to be 100 per cent.

Thinning. Those who do not sow per stations will have to thin rigorously and either waste the plants that are pulled out or transplant them into other prepared beds 6 in. or 9 in. square, depending on the final height of the plants themselves. Never allow the plants to grow in rows thickly, for the final success of a plant is always determined in its early stages.

Planting Out

The plants should be dug up from their nursery beds with as good a ball of soil as possible. They should be transferred to the spot where they are to be planted in shallow trays or boxes, so that the ball of soil does not break away. Good-sized holes should be prepared with trowels so that the roots with their ball of soil around them may fit into their new position with the minimum of disturbance. It is important to water the plants in at this stage and what is known as 'ball watering', i.e. watering round the ball of soil recently inserted to the ground, should be carried out once a day for three or four days after planting if the weather proves dry.

General Remarks

Never allow the biennial to remain in the bed after it has finished flowering. Pull it up and put it on to the compost heap where it can rot down and form manure. Keep the ground well hoed between the plants to eliminate weeds. In dry weather put on top dressings of lawn mowings or other similar material as mulch.

BROMPTON STOCKS. May be described as half-hardy biennials. The plants are erect and have narrow leaves, the edges of which are usually waved. They grow to a height of about 18 in. and flower from June onwards. They may be had as crimsons, mauves, whites or roses.

It is usual to sow the seed in June or July either in the open in a sunny bed or under cloches. Some sow in boxes in the greenhouse though this is really not necessary. Despite thin sowing it is necessary to transplant the stocks when 1 in. high, 4 in. apart. As the stock is very liable to black leg, the soil used in boxes and frames is sterilized or the No-Soil compost is used instead. The plants are finally set out into their permanent beds 9 in. or 1 ft square, and in the north it is usually necessary to cover them with cloches in the winter. Some northern gardeners prefer to leave the plants in the frames until the spring and then plant them out permanently.

Most of the growth of Brompton Stocks is made during the second year and that is the reason why little room need be given to them the first year after sowing. Good varieties are Empress Elizabeth, a large flowered bright rosy carmine. White Lady, a large pure white, and Giant Mauve.

CANTERBURY BELLS. Tall plants that have bell-shaped flowers. They usually grow to a height of 2-3 ft and flower in June, July and August. The seed should be sown at the beginning of May in a sunny spot out of doors under continuous cloches. The land should be enriched with sedge peat at 1 bucketful to the square yard. It is important to sow early, as most of the growth of the canterbury bell is made the first year. Some gardeners sow the seed in boxes in the greenhouse and then when convenient to handle plant out into a finely prepared bed, 6 in. square. Sowing by stations 6 in. apart in a seed bed out of doors saves a great deal of handling and transplanting. If possible the plants should be set out into their flowering positions early in August either 1 ft square or 1 ft by 9 in.

CHEIRANTHUS. This is really the Latin name of the family of wallflower, but is commonly used as the name for the Siberian wallflower Cheiranthus Allionii. This bears beautiful deep orange flowers from May onwards and averages 12 in. high. The seed should be sown in May in the seed bed as advised on page 73. In the north it is advisable to delay the transplanting into the flowering position until March the following year.

EVENING PRIMROSE. There are two main biennial evening primroses, both of which should be sown in seed beds in June or July as advised on page 73. They should then be transplanted in September, and will flower the following summer. Oenothera biennis, the common evening primrose, is the pale yellow fragrant sort that flowers from June to September, and usually grows about 4 ft in height. Golden Yellow is the golden yellow fragrant variety that gives plenty of colour from June to September, and often grows 5 ft tall.

FORGET-ME-NOT. Though usually considered as a blue-flowered plant, it is possible to have pinks and whites. The flowering takes place in April, May or June according to variety, and the flowering stems may be from 12-15 in. long. The seed should be sown in May in the seed bed, as advised on page 73. When station sowing is not practised, handle into further beds 6 in. square. As a result they should grow into quite good plants by October, when they can be planted into their permanent positions. Forget-me-nots appreciate phosphates and potash; work steamed bone flour into the soil where they are to grow at 3 oz to the sq. yard, and give wood ashes if possible at a similar rate.

Good varieties are Royal Blue Re-selected, a very early free flowering deep indigo blue. Marine, a bright blue but not so tall as Royal Blue; and Victoria, a very bright blue, probably the earliest of the three.

FOXGLOVE. A plant that quite likes shade and is often grown in a wild garden or in the margins of shrub borders. There are four biennial border species listed. The seeds are usually sown in a seed bed in a half shady part of the garden early in May. It is important to thin out the seedlings when quite small and transplant them into other borders that have been enriched with peat, so that they may grow on. The planting into their permanent quarters is usually done in September. An interesting variety is Foxy. It grows 3 ft high and is compact and bushy. The flowers are spotted and very attractive. Digitalis gloxiniæflora is the Giant Spotted Foxglove which produces masses of large flowers covered with spots, from July to September on stems 5 ft high. Digitalis monstrosa may be had in various charming colours on stems 4-5 ft tall from July to September. The common Foxglove is Digitalis purpurea which flowers about the same time as the others and grows about 4 ft tall. The flowers are purple.

HOLLYHOCK. There are a few species of hollyhock which are truly biennials and the plants of which may be raised in a similar manner as for wallflowers. The spot where the plants are to grow must be deeply dug and heavily manured because the plant is a deep rooter. Althæa cannabina bears large solitary rose flowers with a yellow base from July onwards, and usually grows about 3 ft tall. A. ficifolia bears pretty yellow and orange flowers in July and August and grows 6 ft high. The common hollyhock that most people know is really a perennial but is usually scrapped after two years for it gets so badly attacked by rust. A dwarf 2 ft variety is Silver Puffs. The flowers are double, fringed and pink. Summer Carnival on the other hand grows 6 ft high and produces double flowers 4 in. across of many differing colours, scarlet, rose, pink, yellow and white.

HONESTY. This, though it has lovely purple blooms, is usually grown for its seed-pods, the centres of which are large, circular and transparent and look like moons. Hence the Latin name Lunaria, from the Latin Luna, the moon. It flowers in May, grows to a height of 3 ft, and the seed should be sown early the previous May out of doors. After thinning, the plants may be allowed to remain there till August when they should be put out into their flowering positions 1 ft apart each way. It is always better to grow Honesty on land that has been manured well for a previous crop. A freshly manured over-rich piece of land tends to encourage too much foliage and too little bloom. The plant will grow quite well in a shady situation. The best variety to grow is the Munstead Purple whose flowers are dark mauve in colour. There is a crimson variety and a white kind as well.

LUNARIA ANNUA   HONESTY

The seed pods make an attractive winter decoration

MULLEIN. The Verbascum. There are over 100 species of mullein but many of them are worthless. There are many good biennials, however, which can all be raised from seed sown in a nice seed bed (see page 73) at any time from mid-April to June. Sow by stations 6 in. apart and transplant into permanent positions in September or the following spring.

Verbascum thapsus is the common mullein, the well-known yellow sort which blooms through the summer and early autumn and may grow to 8 ft high. V. rubiginosum bears yellow flowers deeply tinted with red from June to September and only grows 4 ft high. Verbascum bombyciferum, Arctic Summer, grows 6 ft high and bears spikes of yellow flowers.

SCABIOUS. As the scabious is generally called the Annual Scabious I have included it in the previous chapter. It is however strictly a biennial and may be sown in April or May outside, transplanted in August or September into its permanent position and then flowers in June the following season.

SWEET ROCKET. The plant looks much like an ordinary stock but has hairy toothed leaves. In the country it is often called Dame's Violet. It bears spikes of lilac, or white flowers 3 ft high and is in flower in June and July. The seed should be sown in May or early June in the prepared seed bed as advised on page 73. Sow by stations 6 in. apart and put the plants out in their permanent positions in July or early August, 1 ft square. The blossoms are very richly perfumed, and it is a nice plant to have near the windows of a sitting room.

SWEET WILLIAM. This is strictly a perennial but is invariably grown as a biennial. It flowers in June and early July and can be had in many lovely colours, white, pink, red and mixtures. It generally grows 2 ft tall. The seed should be sown in the seed bed out of doors in May. The plants are set out into their flowering bed in August or September, 1 ft square. The sweet william is happy to grow in almost any soil, and will put up with rather rough treatment. Good varieties are Holborn Glory, a large flowered auricula-eyed strain, and the Unwin Hybrids. The new Extra Dwarf Double Mixed only grows 10 in. high and produces 70 per cent double flowers of beautiful colours.

WALLFLOWER. Few who read this book will not know the wallflower which probably gets its name because it is often found growing naturally in the crevices of old walls. It flowers in April or May growing to a height of 18 in. To get the best plants the seed should be sown thinly in May with the drills 12 in. apart, though those who omit to sow then may put the seed in during June and July. The young plants should be transplanted when 2 in. high into a temporary bed or into their permanent positions. When-

ever they are put out into the spot where they will flower
the distances should be 9 by 9, 12 by 9, or 12 by 12, depending on the size of the plants and the general planning.

It is most important to see that the bed is firm after it
has been dug and manured. Firm soil ensures bushy plants.
Bushiness is also assisted if the growing points are pinched
out when the plants are about 6 in. high. Always plant
with a trowel and never a dibber.

Good varieties are Cloth of Gold, a large handsome yel-
low; Golden Queen, a large flowered deep golden yellow;
Covent Garden Blood Red, a rich velvety crimson; and
Scarlet Emperor, the purest scarlet grown.

The Use of Biennials

Biennials are commonly used in a formal way, that is to say
they are planted out in beds on the square or in some regular formation. This bedding out, as it is called, was particularly popular in the Victorian era and is still very popular
in France and Germany. It is more commonly used in this
country for beds, say in a front garden, or for beds on
terraces. For instance, where tulips are to be planted formally, forget-me-nots are generally planted between, and
thus you get a very bright late spring display.

The great thing is to have a mass of bloom and to put
the plants out so that they have the exact amount of room
they need and no more. The soil is therefore completely
hidden.

Biennials can be used for planting out in drifts in a shrub
border or even in drifts in a herbaceous border. Biennials
do well in narrow borders. I often plant them, for instance,
in a narrow bed I have around the tennis court which is
rather too dry for growing perennials successfully. The
biennial is perfect for the more formal position or the more
formal aspect in the garden.

8 Bulbs and Corms

Bulbs and corms – what a glorious picture they bring to my mind! I can see the drifting mass of bluebells in a wood at Cranbrook; I bring to memory the wealth of yellow and gold of the daffodils in the park land which I used to see in the spring as I drove up to my office at the Cheshire School of Agriculture. I can picture the mass of tulips interplanted with Indigo Blue forget-me-nots which I once tended with care on the terraces of the Swanley Horticultural College and then as I write there comes to my mind the visit paid to a Royal Garden in the north in order to see the baby narcissus only one inch or so high in the rock garden.

Bulbs and corms have a very great part to play not only in the formal beds but in the wilder or more natural parts of the garden. I am going to discuss the planting of the bulbs in the open and intend to use the word bulb to cover corms and on occasion perhaps even tubers. The true bulb when cut across has those layers of flesh which overlap each other in a similar manner to the onion. The true corm such as montbretia or gladioli has a fleshy body and does not consist of a number of layers of flesh like the bulb. It produces a new corm each season, usually above the old one. The tuber is like the potato, being solid and having a number of eyes growing in it. Begonias and anemones are typical tubers treated as bulbs.

Bulbs can be regarded as an investment. If they are treated properly they will last for years. Start by buying good bulbs from a reliable nurseryman. Don't stick to the ordinary kinds of bulbs like the daffodils and tulips. Be ambitious and try some of the more unusual types.

Using Bulbs Formally

Most readers will have seen in parks or big gardens how bulbs can be used in formal beds – square, circular, cut out of the lawn, or surrounded with crazy paving – the sort of beds that you have in a rose garden. In the suburbs formal bedding is very popular in the front garden of the modern house. These beds are usually shaped to suit the outline of the house and are generally planted out on the square system with say, dahlias one foot apart or geraniums at the same distance, or even antirrhinums nine inches square.

When bulbs are used they are usually planted in parallel lines and parallel to the edges of the bed if square or rectangular. When the bed is circular or half-moon shaped,

Lilies

African Marigold F₁
'Diamond Jubilee'

Zinnias

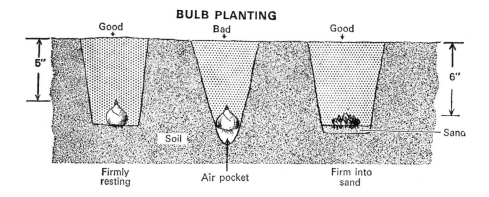

BULB PLANTING

Good · Bad · Good

5" · 6"

Soil · Sand

Firmly resting · Air pocket · Firm into sand

then a diagonal planting scheme is usually adopted. It is never wise to attempt to carry out complicated systems of planting. Stick to one colour and get a really good mass or if you must have more than one colour, arrange for a quarter of the bed to be red, one quarter white, one quarter mauve, and one quarter pink. This is the sort of thing that can be done with tulips. Personally I would never use four colours in this way in one bed. I would much rather use, say, just red and white – either the two opposite quarters red, and vice versa, or else white tulips interplanted with red. The same sort of tricks may of course be played with hyacinths.

In the case of a circular bed it is possible to plant up the centre with a mass of one colour and then to plant another lighter colour in ever-widening circles all round. In the ordinary way, you will arrange to have one type of bulb in one bed but there are exceptions that prove the rule – for instance you can have a centrepiece of an early flowering tulip and the surround could be rows of hyacinths.

This bedding out has to be done properly. Straight lines must be straight lines, or the whole effect looks hideous. Circles must be exactly round and they should radiate from one central point. Spend time in marking the actual spots where the bulbs have to go. See that the right angles are right angles or otherwise when the bulbs come up everyone will see how careless you have been.

Spring Bedding Though bulbs can be used by themselves they always look better when what are called 'carpeting plants' are growing in between. See that the bulbs are planted exactly the same

depth so that they all come up and flower at the same period. Bulbs planted deeper than others flower later and so
spoil the whole effect. Little bulbs like Chionodoxas and
Scillas can be planted 3 in. deep or so around the edge of
a border and left there to come up year after year. I have
planted them around the edges of the beds in my rose garden and the effect in the spring is very pleasing.

Tulips

All kinds of tulips may be used for bedding. There are
those that flower in April and those that bloom later in
May, like the May Flowerers, Cottage and Darwins. Plant
in October in good soil enriched with properly composted
vegetable refuse, dug in a spade's depth, at the rate of, say,
a half bucketful per sq. yard. Fork a good fish manure
into the top 3 or 4 in. at 3 oz to the sq. yard and apply a
top dressing of hydrated lime at a similar rate.

Plant the bulbs 12 in. apart in the rows and 9 in. apart
between the rows. Then put out the carpeting plants in
between (see page 86 for suggestions). There are all kinds
of tulips that can be used but I can recommend the following:

Early Doubles. Madame Testout, a pink; Peach Blossom,
a bright pink; and Marechal Niel, a shaded orange.

Single Earlies. Pink Beauty, a soft pink; Prince of Austria,
a scented scarlet; Marshal Joffre, a bright yellow; and
Brilliant Star.

Paeony Flowerers. Parisian Yellow; Eros, an old rose; Lilac
Perfection; Grand National, a golden yellow; and Orange
Triumph, a bright orange.

Darwins. Bartigon, a bright red; Golden Harvest, a yellow;
Pilgrim, a mauve; Queen of Night, an almost black; and
Clara Butt, a shaded pink.

There are a large number of other varieties that could
be used. Those who are keen will consult the catalogues
of reliable firms and make their own choice.

Daffodils and Narcissus

The name narcissus really includes all the daffodils, but
the man in the street tends to call the daffodil, the one with
the yellow trumpet, and the narcissus the one that bears
smaller flowers either white or yellow. Daffodils on the
whole are not so popular for bedding as tulips or hyacinths,
but when they are used those with the long trumpets are
preferred. Daffodils with shorter trumpets are sometimes

BULBS

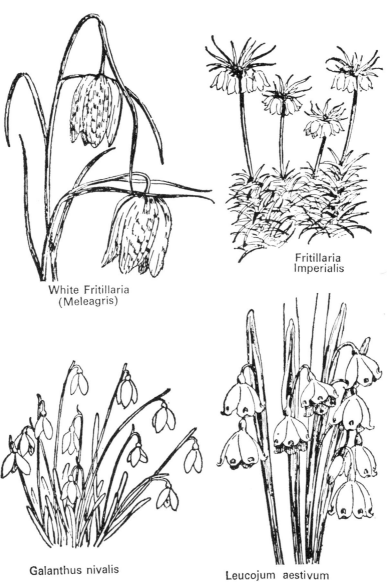

White Fritillaria
(Meleagris)

Fritillaria
Imperialis

Galanthus nivalis

Leucojum aestivum

interplanted with white narcissus and in both cases the beds look at their best when carpeting plants are set out in between.

Varieties that have been used for bedding include Dawson City, a golden yellow flower of perfect shape; Godolphin, with a large widely-expanded trumpet; Beersheba, a white and lemon; Imperator, a pure white of exquisite beauty, Mrs. R. O. Backhouse, commonly called the pink daffodil because the cup is a pale apricot colour turning to pink; Oliver Cromwell, a bi-colour; Victoria with a rich yellow trumpet and pure white petals around; Fortune, with its large orange-yellow cup and clear yellow surround – very early; King Albert, a deep golden yellow, widely flanged; Spanish Gold, a bright celandine yellow; Cheerfulness, the only double Poetaz narcissus, a creamy white with yellow centre; and Actæa, a large Poeticus narcissus with a canary yellow cup edged with red and pure white perianth.

Crocuses

Crocuses are invariably used as edgings and the great advantage is that they can be left in year after year. I have some crocuses myself on either side of a path down by the cordons: they must have been there eight or nine years now and I have never touched them, yet they come up bright and smiling each spring with great success. Plant them two inches apart and about two inches deep. You can always plant violas or pinks in between them or even over them if you wish.

Hyacinths

These are grand bedding bulbs and always look at their best when they are planted close together. The small types may go in as close as six inches square and the taller ones at nine inches square. Never plant the double varieties outside as the flower heads are too weighty when soaked with rain and so tumble to the ground. Tend to buy varieties with short stalks rather than the very tall ones. There is no need for instance to have the top size bulbs. Good seconds are quite good enough. Miniature hyacinths are very pretty indeed. Make a hole with a trowel two inches deep in the case of heavy clay soil and three inches deep in the case of light sandy soil. See that the bottom of the bulb sits firmly in the bottom of the hole and cover it over.

Good varieties to use for bedding are: Ann Mary, an old rose; King of the Blues; Queen of the Whites; City of Haarlem, a deep yellow; Purple King, a rich dark violet; and Lady Derby, a lovely rose pink.

Irises

There are three types of Irises which can be used for bedding. (I am referring of course to the bulbous kinds.) (a) The Dutch, (b) The Spanish, and (c) The English. The Dutch irises flower from mid-May to the end of May and can be bought in various colours – Wedgwood, a lovely blue; White Excelsior, a pure white; Golden Emperor, a deep dark yellow; and Imperator, a deep blue. The Spanish irises flower towards the end of May and can be had in various colours, bearing orange, yellow and purple flowers. The English irises follow the Spanish and are really too late for spring bedding in consequence, but if you do not mind them hanging on late they make a splendid show. There are blue, mauve, white and purple varieties. The Spanish irises should be planted 1½ in. deep, and as close as 3 or 4 in. apart, the Dutch about the same depth and distance, but the English should be planted no deeper than 2 in. and must be 6-8 in. apart. You can space out the Spanish and Dutch irises 9 in. apart if you are going to interplant with forget-me-nots or wallflowers.

General Remarks

Measure the beds up beforehand and work out the exact number of bulbs required as well as the number of carpeting plants you will need. It is always better to order more bulbs than are necessary, so that you can gap up if any should fail.

Plant late in September for daffodils and narcissus, if possible, and some time in October in the case of other bulbs.

Dig the beds over a spade's depth. Bury well-rotted organic matter at the rate of one bucketful per sq. yard in the bottom of the trench. Tread well afterwards to firm and rake the surface level. Before putting in the carpeting plants see that the soil is sufficiently moist and if possible give the plants and good drink before transplanting them.

Start planting the outside rows of the beds and the corners first, working inwards. Stick to a simple scheme, say 6 in. square, 9 in. square or 1 ft square. It is nice to be able to use a plank across the bed to step on, as this prevents heel marks being made. After planting, water well if the weather is dry.

Hoe the beds regularly in the spring when the weeds start to grow. Go over the beds after a frost and firm the plants. Watch out for damage done by strong winds to tall plants. Firm the roots.

For further information on bedding and bedding out see Chapter 9.

Carpeting Plants. A large number of plants can be used for carpeting. I can recommend forget-me-nots, blue, red and mauvish aubretias; double arabis, variegated arabis, polyanthus in different colours, coloured primroses, double daisies, yellow alyssum, and both summer and winter flowering pansies. Those who prefer foliage plants only may use most of the Saxifrages (the prostrate kinds), Veronica repens, some of the Sedums, and the Gibraltar mint.

Naturalizing the Bulbs. Bulbs need not be grown formally in beds. They can be planted naturally in grass or in a wild part of the garden. Generally speaking it is much easier to naturalize bulbs in a large rather than a small garden. I have planted bulbs in a grass orchard, for instance, in a circle around each tree, and then in addition, I have one or two fairy rings of crocuses as well as some drifts of daffodils growing in grass.

If you have got room it is quite a good plan to arrange to have a show for as many months of the year as possible. You start the season with the winter aconites and snowdrops. These are soon followed by scillas and crocuses, and then on to the various types of narcissus and daffodils. Then come the early tulips followed by the Darwin and cottage types, and even later by other varieties. The irises will follow quickly, first the Dutch, then the Spanish and lastly the English. By that time it will be June and many of the lilies will be out together with fritillaries and alliums. The tiger lilies will follow as a rule; then there will be the gladioli. Next come the autumn crocuses and colchicums and lastly the winter flowering cyclamen. All these bulbs will grow in grass, the exception perhaps being the gladioli which prefer to have a little pocket of cultivated soil to grow in.

It is never advisable to plant up the whole of a lawn to bulbs because then it is impossible to mow it and it looks untidy for months. The leaves must always be left to die down naturally so that they can pass back the starches and sugars into the bulbs. By all means plant up grassy banks, the approaches to the lawn, circles round trees, the semi-wild portions of the garden, the drifts on either side or the drive to a house and so on.

Never plant bulbs in grass in straight lines. See that they look natural by planting them in drifts. It is a good plan to take the bulbs and throw them on to the grass and where they fall there they should be planted. In this way they always look more natural. Do the throwing about where you intend the bulbs to be.

A dozen bulbs may look all right in a bowl but plant the same number in a plot of grass 10 ft by 10 ft and the show looks insignificant. It is surprising how many bulbs you need if you are to make a regular splash. Some bulbs like crocuses will be as close as 1 or 2 in. apart, others will be 1 ft away. On a square 10 ft by 10 ft you will probably need 200 daffodils, for instance, to make a good show.

The Planting Operations. Take up the grass by cutting a suitable circle with a trowel, then plant the bulbs from 1-3 in. deep according to its size. The larger bulbs go deeper. Cover with soil, firm, and replace the turf right way up. This is a long job and those who are going in for naturalizing bulbs in a big way had better buy a special turf cutting machine for the purpose. This takes up a circular ring of turf about the size of the bulb to the right depth – automatically. The bulb is then planted in the hole thus made and the turf is pushed back into position very much like a cork being put back into a bottle.

Hedge Banks. If the hedge bank can be kept clean of perennial weeds various bulbs can be planted here with profit. Do not plant them exactly under the hedge or they will not get enough rain, but plant them round the hedge and they will like the protection. The less expensive daffodils, snowdrops, hardy cyclamen, colchicums, and ornithogalums should do quite well. Unfortunately the latter spread rather badly and that has given them a bad name.

Bluebell Corner. There is something very fascinating about the blue of the bluebell and if you want your own miniature bluebell wood to go and look at during the month of May, try planting the bulbs in the autumn about 4 in. deep and as close as 6 in. apart. Plant naturally as advised for daffodils; throw the bulbs on to the grass or soil and then plant them exactly where they fall. By the way, see that they are planted point upwards.

Bulb Buying. Always obtain your bulbs from a reliable nurseryman. For planting in the wild garden or naturalizing, it is often possible to get special mixtures. Such bulbs usually sell at cheaper rates than those for bowls or bedding.

Special Wild Garden Bulbs. Scillas do quite well in the wild garden, especially varieties like Myositis, a blue, Mount Everest, a white, and Azalea, pink. They spread quickly and for this reason some gardeners like to dig them up every 4 years and replant them. They prefer being in a woodland part of the garden rather than in the thick grass of a lawn.

Trillium, the wood lily, will do well in the moister shady parts, and Solomon's Seal, though not a true bulb, loves a shady or partially shady place. The Lily of the Valley is sometimes used in the transition strip between a carefully cultivated area of garden and a wilder plot. This is not a true bulb either, but it likes partial shade.

General Instructions re All Bulbs

In the earlier part of the chapter we have dealt specifically with the use of bulbs for bedding and naturalizing. Now we must examine each type of bulb more carefully and learn more about them.

Narcissi (Daffodils)

There are six main groups of narcissus, the family name of the daffodils: (1) The Trumpets, (2) The Incomparabilis, (3) The Barrii, (4) The Leedsii, (5) The Cyclamineus or Baby Group, and (6) The Triandus, those on short stems. The Barrii and Leedsii groups are often confused, and it should be explained that in the case of the Leedsii group the cups are short and may be white, cream, orange, citron or apricot, but the petals that surround are always white, while in the case of the Barrii the flowers have their cups less than one-third the length of the petals and they are usually tinted with red or orange margins, while the petals that surround them are usually lemon, cream or yellow.

The daffodil does well when naturalized – the baby types flourish in the rock garden; ordinary varieties do well as cut flowers; in fact, they are invaluable in the flower garden. They grow satisfactorily on a wide range of soils and they seem to ask but one thing and that is shelter from wind. Whenever they are to be planted the ground must be perfectly drained. Cultivate deeply and see that all perennial weeds are removed. Most people plant the bulbs 3 in. deep, though large Emperors may be put 4 or 5 in. down. No bulb can ripen properly if planted too deeply. The distance apart varies from variety to variety and as far as the narcissus are concerned the bulbs may be almost touching each other with the rows 9 in. apart. When naturalizing they will be planted as advised on page 87.

When grown as cut flowers it is important not to cut too much foliage as it is the leaves that manufacture the plant food that in turn feeds the bulbs. It is a good plan when flowering is over to tie the foliage in a knot. This keeps it tidy and enables cultivation to be done between the rows. When lifting has to be done the bulbs should be got up as soon as the tops have died down and before any new root development takes place.

Hyacinths

The hyacinth is the ideal bulb for the formal bed or for the bowl. There are some thirty species, most of which have come from South Africa. They can be grown in shrub borders or among evergreens and they mix quite well with other bulbs that flower about the same time.

Hyacinths are usually divided into five groups : (1) Bedding, (2) Exhibition or Potting, (3) Roman or Miniature, (4) The Prepared and (5) The Prepared Miniature. We are not concerned with most of these sections as they are dealt with fully in my book *The Complete Greenhouse Grower*. It is the bedding hyacinths with which we will now deal.

Hyacinths will grow in almost any soil except the badly drained spots. They seem to prefer light land. Those who wish to plant in heavy soil should add horticultural peat beforehand at one bucketful per sq. yard. Hyacinths are sun loving so never plant them in the shade. Give them shelter against strong winds for they are easily beaten down. Dig the ground over a spade's depth and bury well-rotted vegetable refuse, thoroughly decomposed farmyard manure, or horticultural peat at the rate of one bucketful per sq. yard. Fork into the top inch or so bone meal at three oz to the sq. yard, plus a good fish manure at a similar rate.

Plant in September, and to help the root system to form before the hard winter sets in, cover the surface of the ground with a mulching of peat and plant the smallest bulbs 2 in. down and the largest as deeply as 3 in. The lighter the soil the deeper the planting. The bulbs should be 3 in. apart, though the larger ones may be 4 in. apart. When bedding the bulbs will be planted to fit in with whatever scheme is evolved. Always see that the base of the bulb is actually resting on the soil and in heavy land it is worth while putting a little sprinkling of sand in the bottom of the hole in which the base of the bulb can sit.

There are many kinds of Dutch hyacinths that can be used for bedding – white, red, pink, blue, lavender, mauve, purple, yellow and orange. The hyacinth multiflora are quite attractive; they have undergone a special treatment that causes them to throw up twelve or more loosely arranged spikes plus extra foliage.

Tulips

There are hundreds of types of tulips to choose from, singles, doubles, those with blotched flowers, feathery kinds, striped types and so on. I like to divide tulips arbitrarily into five groups: (1) Early Flowering, (2) The Mendels and Triumphs, (3) The Darwins, (4) The Old Fashioned tulips and (5) The Tulipa species. Tulips are very popular for bedding but they look well, too, when planted in clumps or drifts in a shrub border. Mauve coloured tulips, for instance, look well growing among lilacs. Tulips however are not the best of naturalizers and though they will put up with grass, they always prefer to grow in cultivated soil.

They are not particular as to the type of soil in which they grow but they hate waterlogged conditions. Prepare the ground properly as advised for hyacinths (see page 89) and see that the drainage is perfect. Plant the bulbs in October, or if they arrive earlier, late in September. Plant the early varieties 3-4 in. deep, the later varieties say, 6 in. down. The larger the bulb on the whole, the deeper it is possible to plant. The Kaufmannianas are usually planted 8 in. deep except for in the case of very heavy soil. The bulbs can be as close as 6-7 in. apart except in the case of parrot tulips, which because they are shy bloomers had better go in 4 in. apart. See that the bulbs are carefully bedded in the bottom of the hole, carefully dug out with a trowel, and firm the ground well over the top.

Most tulips are lifted annually and once the bulbs have dried off properly they are replanted in a similar position.

Never allow the seed pods to develop but do let the leaves die down naturally so that all the plant food in them may be passed back to the bulbs. The Kaufmannianas and Persicas should never be disturbed.

The early flowering tulips, both single and double, flower in April and May. The Darwins, breeders, double late and single late tulips, flower in May, the Mendel and Triumph tulips usually flower at the end of April and early May and the old-fashioned English tulips like the Bizarres, Rembrandts and Parrots flower late in May, followed as a rule by the Tulipa species.

There are a very large number of varieties, so please consult a good bulb catalogue.

Gladioli

These can be divided into three groups, the early flowering, Primulinus, and Grandiflora or large-flowering type. They are all used for bedding, with fairly tall plants growing in between. They are also used as cut flowers. The Primulinus and the Primulinus Hybrids are lighter in appearance and are excellent for vases for they last so long in water. You often get more than one spike from a corm which you never do in the case of Grandiflora. The Primulinus has a hooded form of top petal while the Grandiflora has the top petal of each flower growing up straight.

Plant Gladioli in a fairly sheltered place and choose a soil that does not dry out too easily. Prepare the ground as advised for hyacinths. Try to get the cultivation done early because the gladioli do not like fresh manure or freshly cultivated soil. In the south plant about mid-March and in the south-west even earlier but in the cold parts of the north delay planting till early in April. Plant the larger corms 4 in. deep with the smaller ones 3 in. deep. In heavy soil sit the corm in a little sand placed in the bottom of the hole. The corms may be planted as close as 3-4 in. apart but when planting in the flower border they will be usually 7 or 8 in. apart. Young well-rounded corms with a high crown usually flower earlier that a flat corm.

Hoe regularly between the gladioli and give liquid manure when the flowers are starting to develop. Mulch with sedge peat in the summer should the weather be dry; each year in October when the foliage is beginning to turn colour, dig the corms up and store in a dry, frost-proof shed.

When the leaves have died down completely clean the corms, remove the leaves, and store.

There are large numbers of Grandiflora, Primulinus and Butterflies, the flower colours varying from dark blue, through violet blue, dark scarlet, to crimson, salmon, pale pink, primrose and pure white. In the case of the Early Flowering gladioli, there are two main groups, the G. Colvillei and the G. Nanus. The Colvillei is a rose, and the Bride a white and in the Nanus Group there are at least three different such as Blushing Bride, Nymph and Peach Blossom.

Irises

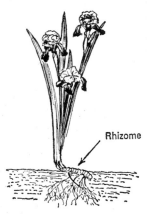

Rhizome

FLAG IRIS

Normally irises prefer light soils but the English varieties do best in the heavier lands. Prepare the ground as advised for hyacinths (see page 89). Plant the bulbs in October though in the south it is possible to continue planting in November. In light soils the bulbs may be buried 4 in. deep and in normal land put them 3 in. down only.

Though the bulbs may be planted so as to almost touch one another (they are often put in this way for the cut flower trade), the gardener will normally have them about 6 in. apart. A hole may be made with a dibber at the right depth and the bulbs dropped in. Where numbers are to be planted in a group it is probably quicker to take out a spadeful of soil 3 in. deep then place the bulbs underneath in the most 'natural' way and put the soil back again, firming it with the back of the spade. Always keep the land clean round about irises.

In the Dwarf Group of irises there are a number of treasures : histroides, a blue purple, white and yellow, which only grows 1 ft high; reticulata, a violet-purple, and reticulata Cantab, a light blue both of which are only 6 in. high. Then there is I. bracteata, a 6-in. yellow and purple, and I. persica, a 2-in. white, green-blue and purple orange type. There are others, of course, but these are my favourites. Those I like best in the Dutch irises are Imperator, a violet-blue; Lemon Queen and White Excelsoir. In the Spanish irises I can recommend Le Mogol, a bronze; King of the Blues; Canary Bird, a primrose; and Cajanus, a canary yellow. In the English iris group, it is best to buy a mixture.

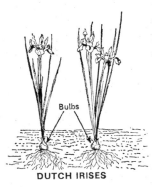

Bulbs

DUTCH IRISES

Anemones

There are four main types of 'bulbous' anemones : St. Brigid, the French, the Fulgens, and the Dutch. The De

Caen differs from the St. Brigid in that the latter are semi-double as a rule and not quite so robust. The St. Brigids are the favourite for garden work. Anemones are a very good cut flower and do quite well in a border in the sheltered parts of the garden. The apennina, blanda and nemorosa types are often grown in the rock garden or planted in the wild garden.

The Anemones do best in medium soil and they love plenty of fine organic matter. It always pays to fork in finely divided leaf mould or sedge peat at a bucketful per sq. yard. Anemones do not object to slight shade and if early blooms are required give them a warm sheltered spot. Work the ground thoroughly before planting and see that it is clean and free from perennial weeds. Dig in organic manure as advised for hyacinths, and give a similar dressing of organic fertilizers.

Plant in October or early November for flowering in March or early April or plant in February or March for flowering from the end of August onwards. It is possible in the south at any rate to have them flowering in December and January if the anemone rows are covered with cloches. The Rock Garden and Wild Garden types are usually planted in October, though in cold parts of the north it is worth while delaying planting till the spring. Don't plant deeper than 2 in. in the case of the larger corms, and only 1 in. with the smaller ones. The soil should not be dry at the time of planting. It is usual to arrange the rows 14 in. apart for the taller types and 12 in. apart for the shorter ones. Cut flower growers often plant 9 in. apart between the rows and 2 in. apart between the corms. See that the corms are properly bedded into the ground and in the north it is worth putting bracken or pea sticks over the top in winter and early spring to break the wind and frost. Cloches are even better.

It is possible to raise St. Brigid anemones by sowing seed in July for flowering the following spring or by sowing in February under cloches for flowering in late autumn.

Rananculus
The Turban Ranunculus look something like pom-pom dahlias when growing. The Persians, another type, are very susceptible to weather damage. They all like a soil rich in peaty humus and they prefer a warm south border. Plant the tubers with their claws downwards 2 in.

deep and 6 in. apart. Plant in the autumn, and the flowers will be out in May. Delay planting till March in the north and blooming will take place from June onwards.

Lilies

There are some four hundred species, or so-called species, of the Lily family and I always feel that there are many more types and kinds than that. Naturally some lilies are very delicate and are therefore only suitable for the greenhouse. Many of them grow well among shrubs, particularly rhododendrons. Others prefer the wild garden, for instance, L. superbum, while the smaller types like L. tenuifolium look very attractive in the rock garden. Lilies grow in all types of soils, providing they are well drained. The American species like a peaty soil. Liliums tigrinum, candidum, croceum, and elegans like a heavier soil. Those with rather damp soil will have to concentrate on L. superbum and canadense, but even these do not like sitting in stagnant water. Soils which contain a fair amount of natural chalk or limestone are only suited to certain lilies like the Martagon lilies and the candidums.

All lilies like shelter and most of them seem to do quite well in partial shade. Don't plant them too close to the shrubs or the roots will take away all the moisture. Dig plenty of sedge peat or compost into the ground where lilies are to be planted and when specimens are to be grown, dig out a hole 18 in. deep and a similar width and length. Bury a few brickbats in the bottom and then mix up a compost consisting of 1 part soil, 1 part sedge peat and 1 part sand, and put into the hole. Bone meal should be added at the same time 4-5 oz to the sq. yard.

It must be remembered that lilies will remain in position for years and so careful preparation takes time but is worth it. Most lily bulbs are imported and usually arrive in time for the autumn planting. Plant as soon as you receive the bulbs. This will mean November for the dormant ones and March for those that have to be brought on in frame. The depth of the planting differs according to the size of the bulbs, but a general guide is to plant them so that they are about three times as deep as their greatest diameter. Place a little sand below the bulb at planting time, so as to make certain of draining away any surplus moisture and so prevent the bulb from rotting.

Bulbs of the non-stem-rooting kinds may remain dormant

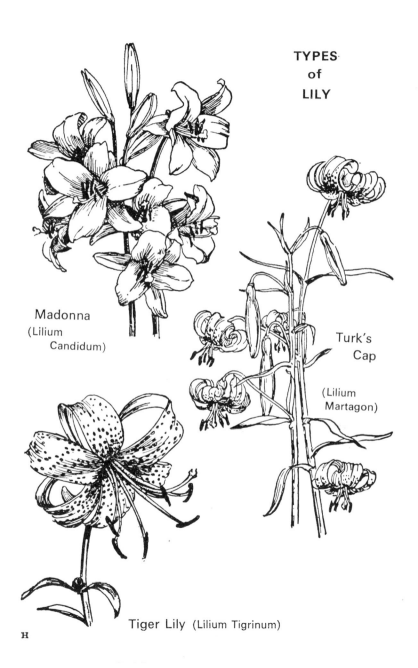

TYPES of LILY

Madonna
(Lilium
Candidum)

Turk's
Cap

(Lilium
Martagon)

Tiger Lily (Lilium Tigrinum)

H

a whole season after planting and will not begin to show until the second summer. This holds good whether planting is done in the autumn or spring. The stem-rooting kinds usually bloom the first summer. The small growing kinds like L. tenuifolium may be planted as close as 6 in. but the taller varieties should be at least 1 ft apart.

Mulch in the summer by putting on top dressings of damped sedge peat to a depth of 2 in. Stake the taller ones with a bamboo if they become too top heavy. Feed in the summer with liquid manure, giving three applications at fortnightly intervals as the lilies come into bloom.

There are so many varieties to choose from that it is impossible to do more than mention a few. The outside lilies can be divided into three groups, the Early Flowering, Mid Season and Late. In the Early Group I can recommend Martagon the deep purple, Golden Gleam the apricot yellow, and the Madonna lily. In the Mid Season Group I should like to have Regale, Sulphurgale and Superbum a reddish orange. In the Late Group there is that vigorous grower The Tiger Lily, Auratum, the white with the gold band through each petal, and Henryi with rich orange yellow flowers. Auratum needs planting 1 ft deep.

For fuller details of the different varieties see a good bulb catalogue.

Crocuses

One of the easiest and hardiest bulbs to grow. Never cut the leaves off but tie the foliage in a knot after the flowers have faded, to make them look neater. Crocuses make a good edging plant to a border; they look well in a shrubbery, and are grand for naturalizing in grass. They will grow in almost any soil and should be planted 3 or 4 in. deep and 2-3 in. apart. Plant as soon as the bulbs become available in October. See that they are well buried down in the soil and when planting look out for any soft decaying bulbs and see that these are burnt.

There are spring and autumn flowering crocuses and there are a number of named varieties which usually bloom early. I can recommend Blue Peter, a medium blue; Mary, a dark blue; Snow White, a pure white; Ruby Giant, a dark purple; and Zwanenburg, a yellow.

Grape Hyacinths (Muscari)

These come into flower soon after crocuses. They naturalize quite well in a woodland garden. They look beautiful in the shrub border if planted in drifts and to get a good blue haze effect you need about 50 bulbs in a group. They like rather open soil with plenty of sand or grit in it and the heavier soils may be enriched with such material. Plant late September or early October, 3 or 4 in. deep and as close as 3-4 in. apart. Mulch the bulbs with a little horticultural peat or leaf mould for the first year or two.

There are a number of varieties, but the most popular one today is known as Heavenly Blue.

Scillas (Bluebells)

The scillas and squills are in the same family. The squill is really a dwarf kind of Scilla sibirica and the Bluebell a tall kind of Scilla festalis or S. nutans. They are a family that will flower almost anywhere. They seem as happy in shade as in sunshine. They grow in banks or under trees, but to look well they must be planted in a mass. The Bluebells grow about 1 ft high and the squills not more than 3 or 4 in. high. Neither of them like to be disturbed so they can be left down for years and years. There are pink and white types of Bluebells but it is the blues that are most popular.

Plant early in September if possible. Normally the right depth, especially in light soil, is 5-6 in. but for Siberica 3 in. will do. The squills if planted no deeper than this will flower with the Crocus and Bluebells.

Snowdrops

These are almost the first bulbs to bloom and as they dislike being disturbed they should be left for years after planting. They are easy to grow and so do well in almost all soils. Plant them in the wild garden, plant them in the orchard, grow them alongside the paths, have little groups if you will in front of the herbaceous border, but to get the best effects always have 20-30 bulbs together. On the whole, snowdrops prefer a light soil and if planting in very heavy clay add horticultural peat at a bucketful per sq. yard.

Plant the bulbs 3 in. deep and as close as 1 in. if you wish. Naturally when planting in drifts some bulbs will be 4-5 in. apart and others much closer together. Get the planting done as soon as the bulbs are on sale, or arrive.

Galanthus nivalis is the common snowdrop; G.n. flore pleno a double and pretty at that. G. Elwesii is the giant snowdrop best grown in cultivated land.

Winter Aconites   The winter aconites belong to the buttercup family and do well in a half shady place, in the wild garden and in shrub borders. They are very hardy and spread quickly. They produce clear bright yellow blooms soon after the snowdrop. The bulbs should be planted 2-3 in. deep in moist rather than drier soil. The usual Aconite grown is Eranthis hyemalis.

Leucojum (Snowflake)   Looks very much like the snowdrop and is often mistaken for it. It bears white flowers with green tips on stems 7 or 8 in. tall. The bulbs should be planted 3 in. deep in well-drained soil. They love a sloping bank. The best known is Leucojum vernum.

Camassia   This bears attractive star-shaped blossoms either light blue, purplish blue or white, depending on variety. It thrives in shade as much as in the open. Plant the bulbs 4-5 in. deep and 3-4 in. apart. They do quite well in a heavy soil. The flowers usually appear in May, or as late as early June. Camassia esculenta looks rather like a large blue hyacinth.

Allium   A member of the onion family. Most varieties flower in May or June and my favourite, A. Moly, is at its best at the end of May producing a mass of yellow flowers on stems 1 ft high. Do not plant in grass. They prefer cultivated land. Plant the bulbs 2-3 in. apart. A. acuminatum bears rose coloured flowers on stems 8 in. high and A. neapolitanum bears pretty white flowers with really lovely glossy dark green foliage below.

Sternbergias   This is an autumn flowerer and produces its blooms long before the leaves. It quite likes a heavy soil and prefers a somewhat shady position. It grows rather like a large crocus, sending up several bright yellow flowers at a time. It hates lime, so do not plant in a chalky soil. Plant in August, burying the bulbs 3-4 in. deep and 6 in. apart. Fork sedge peat or leaf mould into the soil beforehand at 1 bucketful per sq. yard. It is a very good edging plant.

Autumn Crocus   This is a surprisingly lovely flower which is at its full beauty in September and October. The lovely crocus-like blooms appear first and the large strap-like foliage afterwards.

Always plant in July if you can and never delay after the middle of August. Autumn crocuses do well in grass and are just as happy growing in front of the herbaceous border in a clump or drift. They look well planted in circles around trees in an orchard. There are a large number of types, my favourites being Crocus medius, a lavender purple feathered purple; C. longiflorus, a lilac; and C. Talzmanni, a scented lavender blue.

9 Plants for Bedding Out

Bedding may be described as a system of planting certain types of plants that will give bloom at a certain time of the year or to cover a certain period. Sometimes shrubs are used – sometimes small trees – other times hardy and half hardy annuals – biennials – perennials – greenhouse plants and, of course, bulbs.

Bedding can either be of a permanent nature, i.e. the shrubs or perennials like Pæonies, or of a temporary character, like Wallflowers or sub-tropical plants which cannot be planted till June and cannot last longer than the end of September.

The permanent type costs more to start with but less afterwards. The temporary type entails less initial expense – but takes far more labour.

Bedding out was far more popular in Victorian days because it had a certain formality about it and also because it ensued colour for long periods – in those days time and cost of labour were of little consequence! They went in for carpet bedding – intricate geometric design – with special plants which were kept dwarf by being pinched back every week. Today bedding is usually of one colour alone – shown up perhaps by foliage plants.

Formal bedding is suited particularly to (a) borders against the house (b) beds or borders on terraces (c) beds in lawns, (d) beds in the front garden, (e) beds in a formal garden with crazy paving around, (f) beds in a small garden in towns and cities.

Preparing the Beds

When raking to make the bed level, work in a good fish manure at 3-4 oz per sq. yard or use 'meat and bone meal' instead. Most good fish manures are prepared with a little extra potash added and so it is not necessary to add this 'ingredient'. In the case of the meat and bone meal it is advisable to use sulphate of potash at 2 oz to the sq. yard in addition, if available, or finely divided wood ashes at about $\frac{1}{2}$ lb. per sq. yard instead.

The beds must be well trodden to get them firm, and it may be convenient to do this before the levelling. In the case of lumpy soil it is advisable to rake, tread and rake again. Plant in showery weather if possible. In a droughty period put an overhead sprinkler in position so that with the tap turned on and the whirling spray, and the necessary hose, you can ensure that the beds get a really good soaking with water applied in its fine aerated state. See that the plants that you are going to move are watered the day before, and always transplant them with a good ball of soil to their roots if you can.

Plant the outside rows of the bed first in the corners and then work towards the middle. The distances vary from plant to plant but normally speaking 1 ft square is ideal with perhaps bulbs at 6 in. in between. Rake the ground level afterwards and after that all that will be necessary is occasional hoeing, though in the case of plants set out in October it may be necessary to firm them in again after a bad frost in November or December. In the case of the summer bedding this will not be necessary.

Spring Bedding Plants

WALLFLOWERS. These will be sown in June or July in the reserve garden in rows 1 ft apart. Thin the plants out early and transplant them 1 ft apart. Pinch the tip of the main growth out to make the plants bushy. Hoe regularly throughout the summer. There are dwarf wallflowers 9 in. high and taller ones like Fire King, 15 in.; Primrose Monarch 18 in.; and Blood Red, 15 in.

The Siberian Wallflower or Cheiranthus allionii grows 12 in. high. It is bright orange and is very popular. It is usually sown in July as if sown earlier it tends to bloom in the autumn.

There are double wallflowers but they are not quite hardy and are usually propagated by cuttings taken in August. As they are heavy and need staking they are not so popular as the ordinary varieties.

Remember all wallflowers need lime as they are subject to Club Root Disease.

FORGET-ME-NOTS. These have the advantage of flourishing in shade and will even do well under trees. There are varieties that differ in height from 6-12 in. and the colours vary from deep to pale blue. Sow in June or July in a shady border in rows 9 in. apart. Thin out to this distance, and as a result you ought to get good plants to put out into flower beds in September or October. Royal Blue is 12 in. high; Marine, 9 in. high.

AUBRIETIA. Very useful for carpeting the ground. Looks very lovely with bulbs. Can be had in mauve, blue or crimson. Usually propagated by cuttings taken in August in a cold frame. Aubrietia prefers a dry position in full sun.

Good varieties are Dr. Mules, a purple, and Fire King, a crimson.

DOUBLE ARABIS. Grows 6 in. high. Succeeds well in light soil. Propagate in light soil by cuttings in August. On heavier soil take cuttings in June or July. There is a variegated variety with striped yellow leaves but it is less robust than the normal kind.

POLYANTHUS. Quite lovely in beds alone, or can be interplanted with bulbs. They bloom in April and May. Can be propagated by seed sown in a frame or under cloches in February, the plants being pricked out in a reserve border in April 9 in. apart. After flowering, the plants may be taken up and pulled to pieces and planted in the reserve 9 in. apart. They then make quite good plants for next autumn's bedding out. The Munstead strain is very good.

COLOURED PRIMROSES. Propagate as for polyanthus. Never discard weak-looking plants. They often throw the best colours. Blackmore and Langdon have a very good strain.

DOUBLE DAISIES. Make compact dwarf plants good good for an edging. They are hungry feeders and tend to starve the ground in which they grow. Sow in May or June in a warm sunny border. Prick out 6 in. apart and plant out in flowering beds in the autumn for blooming in the spring. After flowering they may be split up for planting in the reserve.

YELLOW ALYSSUM. Grows 8 in. high and has greyish green leaves with lovely yellow flowers. Propagate by seed sown in April and in the Reserve. Flowers rather late and very useful for growing under late flowering tulips.

WINTER FLOWERING PANSIES. Can be had in colours white, yellow and blue. Sow seed in July, plant in main beds in autumn. Should flower through a mild winter as well as giving a good display in the spring.

The 'In-Between' Bedding

Plants too late for Spring Bedding but a little too early for summer bedding.

SWEET WILLIAMS. Usually sown in May in a nice seed bed and then pricked out 9 in. square in the reserve plot. The plants are then put out in their flowering beds in the autumn or early spring. They are in flower in May and early June. They can be had in pink, crimson, or magenta, with or without white eyes. Grow 18 in. high. **After flower-ing** the plants should be thrown on to the compost heap.

CANTERBURY BELLS. Sow early in May as advised for Sweet Williams. Thin and plant out in the reserve plot 1 ft apart. In the normal way they are rather tall for bedding, often growing 3 ft in height. They will however, put up with shade. It is possible to get single, double cup and saucer varieties in shades of pink, mauve or white. Tall plants need staking.

Bulbs Suitable for Spring Bedding. The fullest details re bulbs will be found in the bulb chapter. As far as beds and bedding are concerned they can be used by themselves or better still, with carpeting plants below them. I have sometimes used hyacinths, anemones and chionodoxas as permanent bedding bulbs. They have to be planted fairly deeply so that the shallow rooting summer flowering plants can grow quite well over the top, and round about them. Be sure to plant all the bulbs the same depth so that they all flower together.

The best bulbs to use for bedding are :

TULIPS. Early and late flowering singles and doubles for April. Single May flowering, cottage and Darwins for May.

LINING OUT HARD WOOD CUTTINGS

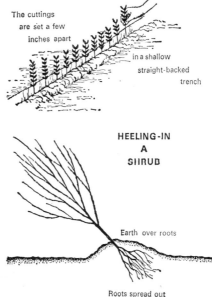

The cuttings are set a few inches apart

in a shallow straight-backed trench

HEELING-IN A SHRUB

Earth over roots

Roots spread out

Aim to plant in October; remove after flowering and plant in reserve till foliage dies down.

NARCISSUS. This includes all daffodils and narcissus. Plant in September, as root action starts early.

ANEMONE. Useful for carpeting under more permanent shrub bedding.

CHIONODOXAS. Grows 7 in. high. A beautiful blue.

CROCUS. Usually used as edgings. Can be planted with pinks and violas to flower over them.

SCILLAS and *MUSCARI.* Useful under more permanent shrub bedding. Glorious blue.

HYACINTHS. Look better planted close together, 6-9 in. apart so that they hold each other up. Single hyacinths are better than doubles. Buy medium size bulbs which will produce one good bloom.

IRISES. Dutch, colours blue, white and yellow. Flower mid to end May. Spanish, yellow, orange, bronze, blue, purple. Flower end May early June. English, blue, mauve, white, purple. Flower early June.

Suggested Forms of 'Shrub' Spring Bedders. When dealing with bulbs, reference has been made to the more permanent shrub bedding. Any of the flowering shrubs may be used for this purpose, with the bulbs acting as carpeters beneath. Buy the dwarf varieties of the shrubs mentioned. Any good nurseryman will advise and help you in this matter.

Azaleas, Daphnes, Hamamelis, Baby Rhododendrons, Flowering Cherries.

Spring Bedding Schemes I Have Admired. 1. A single yellow tulip carpeted with Forget-me-nots. 2. A bronzy-purple tulip carpeted with a reddy bronze Wallflower. 3. A double early tulip carpeted with a purple Aubrietia. 4. Good pink hyacinths carpeted with white flowered winter flowering pansies.

Summer Bedding or 'In-Between' Bedding

There are a large number of plants for summer bedding which should give you a good show from June to October. Some are grown because of the flowers themselves, others because of their brightly coloured leaves. Occasionally plants may be introduced to give height. These are usually known as 'dot' plants. You may have just one central one, or four dotted about at even distances in the beds.

It is not usually necessary to prepare the ground especially well for summer bedding. Just remove the spring bedding plants. Fork over shallowly, working in sedge peat at a bucketful per sq. yard, plus a good fish manure at 3 oz to the sq. yard. If the soil is dry, and it often is at this time, the peat should be damped first of all. Tread the soil to make it firm and rake it to level.

Summer Bedding Plants

CHINA ASTERS. Flower early August-October.

LARKSPURS. Flower July-September. Two colours, rose scarlet and deep blue go well together.

LOBELIA. Flower all the summer. Buy plants or raise in the greenhouse.

NASTURTIUMS. Flower all the summer. Use dwarf varieties.

NEMESIA. 6-9 in. high. Flower all the summer. One of the loveliest bedding plants there is. Can be had as blue or orange and red mixed.

PETUNIAS. August-October. Single varieties are best. Look well in beds alone or interplanted with Phlox Drummondii.

PRUNING

A covering of white lead or tar will prevent bleeding and serve as a protection against disease

LAYERING

A little sand scattered around the split portion of the stem will encourage rooting.

PREPARING A 'HEEL' CUTTING

Suitable side shoot is stripped off with a 'heel' of older wood and trimmed

SHIRLEY POPPIES. Flower all the summer. Easy to grow. Sow seed in position.

ICELAND POPPIES. August-October. Raise seed as for Canterbury Bells (see page 103).

PHLOX DRUMMONDII. All the summer. Grows very quickly from seed. Separate colours or mixed. Only one inch high, if you peg it down. Does well on dry soil.

STOCKS (10 weeks). Flower June and July. Sow early March in greenhouse or under cloches. *East Lothian,* flower July and August. Sow in March in greenhouse or under cloches. More robust than 10 weeks stocks.

ZINNIAS. Flower July-end September. Sow in March under cloches or in greenhouse. Like sheltered warm position and rich soil. Excellent when sown in situ under lantern cloches.

ANTIRRHINUMS. Flower all the summer. Were the most popular of all bedding plants until the disease, Rust, appeared. Seed usually sown in early spring under glass. Seedlings must be transplanted before they become drawn. Pinch plants when a few inches high, to make them bushy. Convenient to use bedding varieties because these have compact growth.

BEGONIAS. Fibrous rooted. Flower all the summer. Sow seed in greenhouse in January by sprinkling it on damp soil. Seed is so small it must not be covered. Transplant seedlings when small. Plant out in beds early in June. Plants can be lifted in autumn and boxed up and kept in a warm greenhouse throughout the winter. Cuttings are usually taken in the spring.

BEGONIAS. Tuberous rooted. Tubers are usually purchased and are started into growth by being planted shallowly in boxes of leaf mould or fibre in February. The plants are then potted up as soon as they have started to grow and so are ready to be planted out early in June after hardening off. There are both single and double varieties. The tubers may be kept from year to year in a greenhouse after they have been 'ripened off'.

SALVIAS. Flower all the summer. One of the most brilliant scarlet flowering plants. Excellent for bedding. Sow seed in February in warm house. Transplant seedlings early and eventually pot up into 6-in. pots. Put out into their flowering position the third week of May.

CALCEOLARIAS. Flowering July-late September. Can

be had in yellow, bronze and red. Cuttings are usually taken in October in a frame.

PENTSTEMONS. Flower end June-end September. Good because they like a wet season! Take cuttings in September and October from base of plant. Strike in cold frame and keep there throughout the winter. Plant in beds in early April.

VIOLAS. Flower all the summer. Cuttings taken in September and October, struck in cold frame in light sandy soil. A good way of getting cuttings is to cut the plants hard back after flowering and put a handful of leaf mould in the centre of each plant. May be had in mauves, blues, yellows, whites, and other colours. Keep cutting off the dead blooms – or the plants will cease to flower.

DAHLIAS. Flower all the summer. One of the most popular bedding plants today. Dwarf types are particularly useful, as are Miniature Cactus types. Plant after the middle of May when fear of frost is over.

FUCHSIAS. Flower late summer to end September. Very graceful bedding plants. Large beds may be varied with dwarf specimens, or taller 'trees'. There are a large number of excellent varieties. Do not plant out until the beginning of June. Propagate by cuttings taken in autumn or spring in a warm greenhouse.

HELIOTROPE. Flowers late summer-end September. A lovely scented plant. Often grown as dwarf bushes but can be had as half-standards like fuchsias.

GERANIUMS. Flower all the summer. A very popular bedder. Plant out late in May from 3-in. pots. Usually propagated by cuttings taken in August or September in the greenhouse. Paul Crampel the single scarlet, and Gustav Emich the most popular varieties but King of Denmark, a double salmon, is also very good.

The following are a few of the foliage plants that are used in bedding :

PYRETHRUM aureum, the golden feather plant. Raised from seed sown in heat early in the spring.

COLEUS has crimson purple leaves; take cuttings in spring.

AMARANTHUS, purple and red leaves. Sow in greenhouse in spring.

IRESINE, crimson leaves, take cuttings in the spring.

ANTENNARIA or Cat's ear, a very dwarf plant. A perennial, so propagate by division in autumn or spring.
SANTOLINA. Grey finely cut leaves; propagate by cuttings in cold frame in autumn.

Flowers are not only lovely in a garden but beautiful in the house. One of the features of our British households is surely that of being able to have bowls of flowers in the living rooms all the year round.

In this chapter I want to deal with the question of growing flowers which the housewife can feel happy about cutting at any time. Too often the husband plans a wonderful herbaceous border and is expecting to see it look at its best – only to find on coming home one evening that the flowers which should be blooming in the border and looking their best, are now adorning a bowl in the drawing room. This 'competition' between the garden and the house can easily be overcome if a small plot of land can be set aside purely for the purpose of growing flowers for cutting. Such a border may be large or small, depending on (a) the size of the gardens and (b) the needs of the house. It should be planted up with rows of annuals, biennials and perennials which give as long a period of flowering as possible. Those who look after their own gardens will probably concentrate on perennials, for these give the minimum of trouble. Thus the succession will probably start with doronicum, and end with Michaelmas daisies.

Standardization　　In this part of the garden the plants will be set out in serried rows. The whole idea is to grow as many flowers as possible in the minimum of space. It should be possible to bend down and cut all the flowers required without actually standing on the flower beds. The scheme I have found most successful is to have four rows 1 ft apart on a 3 ft bed. This is quite possible, though it sounds peculiar, for two rows are on the extreme outside of the bed. Then you have a path 2 ft wide, a 3 ft bed, and so on. The paths need not be gravel or concrete; they are usually just trodden earth. This makes it possible to dig up the whole strip of ground concerned, paths and all, later on, if it is intended to use the ground for some other purpose.

The rows should be run north and south, the beds themselves being no wider than 6 or 8 ft, though in a large garden they can be extended to 20 ft or more. The whole point of having narrow beds with paths between is to enable the womenfolk to cut the flowers in comfort without getting their feet muddy, and without having to tread in and among the plants. With beds of this width it is possible to cut every flower from the paths on either side.

Another advantage of having four short rows like this is that it is quite easy to do all the supporting of the plants needed by pushing bamboo sticks every 6 ft or so around the outside of the bed and stretching string or 'fillis' as it is usually called, in between the bamboos at a height of, say, 2 ft, 3 ft and 4 ft, and in the case of the taller plants like delphiniums and larkspurs, say at 5 ft also. By having these guard surrounds the flower stems as a whole are kept sufficiently upright for cut flower purposes. It is not advisable or necessary to try and stake each plant and you cannot use pea sticks for twiggy sticks get in the way when cutting blooms quickly.

By having standardized beds like this you can cover the beds temporarily with Dutch lights at any time. These frame lights with one pane of glass only in each of them can be held in position by means of a temporary framing of timber. Those who are interested in this particular type of protection can study the matter further in my book, *Cut Flowers for the Home*. Many people like to cover the mid-season varieties of chrysanthemums as this makes it possible to keep out several degrees of frost in October.

Preparation of the Ground

The same care should be taken with the preparation of the ground for the cut flower border as with the herbaceous border. When digging over the ground shallowly in the autumn, properly composted vegetable matter will be incorporated at, say, one good bucketful per sq. yard. Leave the ground so that the frost can act on it. Thus it will be easier to work in the spring, and at that time organic fertilizer like fish manure or meat and bone meal will be worked in at 3 oz to the sq. yard plus wood ashes at 6 oz to the sq. yard.

If it is intended to plant up perennials in the autumn, the ground cannot be left rough for any time. It will have to be firmed and forked down soon afterwards. Lime will be used in all cases, for from the cut flowers point of view there are no lime-haters. Apply it as a top dressing, but do not fork it into the land for it washes through quickly. Use hydrated lime at 4-5 oz to the sq. yard. Where lime-loving plants like scabious and gypsophila are grown, a similar dressing will be given each season.

Annuals as Cut Flowers. Many annuals make excellent cut

flowers, especially those classed as hardy. They like to be grown in a fairly sheltered sunny spot in well-drained soil. It is always important to get the ground prepared a month before sowing so as to allow the land to settle. Annuals may be sown in the spring from March till the end of April, depending on the season and the locality. It is always better where possible to sow in the autumn, say about the middle of September, and thus the plants live through the winter and flower two or three weeks earlier in the summer.

Annuals fit just as easily into the standard scheme of bedding as advised for perennials. The rows will be 1 ft apart and the aim will be to thin the plants out to at least 1 ft apart in the rows. The taller annuals like corn-flowers and Imperial larkspurs may be thinned to 2 ft apart in the rows. Those who go in for station sowing in order to save seed (an excellent plan) will sow three seeds at 1 ft distances along the rows and thin down to one per station should more than one seed grow at that point. All annual seeds must be sown shallowly so the drills need not be drawn out deeper than half an inch.

Hoe regularly between the rows if the mulching method has not been adopted, as weeds have a tendency to smother out the young annuals when they are trying to establish themselves. When the sedge peat or compost mulch is applied no weeds are able to grow. Give a mulching of sedge peat all over the ground. See that the flowers are picked regularly and even if they are not required, remove the flower heads so that the flowering period may be extended. It is always best to pick annuals either early in the morning or late in the evening and then to place them immediately into deep receptacles so that they can be up to their necks in water for two or three hours before being put into vases in the house.

Varieties

The following are suitable for sowing in the autumn: Cornflower, Double Blue and double Atropurpurea, a maroon purple and of good height. Candytuft, in blue, pink and all shades of mauve. Calendula, varieties Camp Fire, the best crimson-orange, Geisha Girl, an orange with incurved petals, and Orange King, a beautiful orange. Larkspur, the stock-flowered strain are tall and branchy, lovely colours, mauve and pink. Love in the Mist (Nigella) Miss

Jekyll, a light blue, Persian Jewels Mixed, various colours.

As the result of September sowings the Cornflower will be ready to cut by the end of May, the Candytuft at the end of June, the Calendula mid June, the Nigella, June.

If the rows are covered with continuous cloches from the middle of December onwards and the cloches removed directly the annuals reach the top of them, it is possible to have cut flowers in each case a fortnight or three weeks earlier.

Varieties that live through the winter in the south :

Annual Chrysanthemum, the good types being Morning Star, Primrose Yellow, Eastern Star, a yellow with chocolate centre, Northern Star, a cream with a yellow border, Princess May, a white single and Coronet, a cream edged with lemon.

Clarkia, which can be had in various colours, carmine, rose, mauve, scarlet-purple and salmon. I like the Pulchella mixed, semi-double flowers in various colours, white, violet and carmine.

Gypsophila. Grow Monarch, the very select strain.

Larkspur. The most handsome are the stock-flowered.

Linaria. Have Maroccana Excelsior, a beautiful mixture.

Saponaria. Grow Vaccaria, rose.

Sweet Sultan. Purchase the seed under guaranteed colours, purple, white or yellow.

The Annual Chrysanthemum flowers in June; Clarkia in May and June; Godetia from mid June onwards; Gypsophila all through the summer, according to the sowings made; the Linaria, June, and the Saponaria in spring and early summer, and Sweet Sultan in July. Again, if these annuals are covered with continuous cloches they will flower two or three weeks earlier.

Half-Hardy Annuals

The half-hardy annuals are those that will not stand any frost at all and are usually sown in boxes or pots. The plants that result are put out in the open after the middle of May when all fear of frost has passed. Latterly many of the half-hardy annuals have been sown under cloches out of doors, the sowings being made early in March in the south and late in March in the north.

China Asters. Usually flower in July and August. May be sown under glass at the end of March in a greenhouse at a temperature of 60 degrees F. or may be sown in a frame and the plants thinned out as soon as they are convenient to handle; the planting out being done in May.

Good varieties are Victoria which can be bought under the colours carmine, white, lilac, etc.

Pæony flowered which can be bought as crimson, rose, light blue, etc., Comet, which has compact growth, in colours of lilac, rose, crimson, white and carmine.

Ostrich Plume, an excellent type available in most colours.

Sinensis, the single or marguerite aster with its crimson violet mauves, pinks and whites.

Single Comet, or as it is often called, Giant Single Chinese Comet.

Stocks. There are two main types of annual stocks, the **Ten Week** and the **East Lothian**. The Brompton Stocks are really biennials and appear in Chapter 7. Even the ones dealt with in this chapter should really go into the biennial group.

The Ten Week stocks grow about 18 in. high and flower in July and August. The seed is usually sown in boxes in the greenhouse in March and the plants thus raised are put out permanently in May. It is possible to sow the seed out of doors under cloches in March, especially if the cloches are put into position over the ground a fortnight before sowing.

The large flowering Ten Week stocks may be obtained in the following colours : light violet, pale lavender, white, deep rose and pure rose.

The East Lothian stocks grow 15 in. high and are usually sown in July or August in frames or open ground in a sheltered position. The plants are then either covered with cloches from October onwards or may be planted out into frames over winter. They are usually allowed to flower where they are grown but it is possible to take the plants out of the frames and plant in the flowering position in May. From August sowings you can get good blooms from May till the end of August the following year. If you delay sowing till February you cannot get flowers to cut until about the end of June.

Zinnias. One of the best cut flowers. In season from August till September. May be had in various colour forms, mostly red, orange, primrose, purple, white and rose. Sow at the end of March in boxes in the greenhouse and plant out at the end of May or better still, sow where the plants are to grow, at the end of March under Access Frames.

COSMOS. Flowers usually in August and September and may grow to a height of 6 ft. Usually sown in March in boxes in the greenhouse or directly into the cut flower border under cloches about mid-March.

Everlasting Flowers

The everlastings make good cut flowers and enable the supply of bloom to be kept up throughout the winter. All the everlastings mentioned in Chapter 6 are suitable for the purpose.

Biennials

The following biennials make good cut flowers : Brompton Stocks, Canterbury Bells, Honesty, Annual or Biennial Scabious, Sweet William, Wallflowers, Forget-me-nots, Sweet Rocket.

Remember the plan in the cut flower border is to keep the bed standardized, so with both the annuals and biennials the rows will be planned 1 ft apart and if any greater distance is needed this should be given in the rows.

Perennials

There are a very large number of perennials that make excellent cut flowers.

The following should certainly be included in the list : Achillea, Alstrœmeria, Aquilegia, Campanula, Coreopsis, Chrysanthemum maximum, Dahlia, Delphinium, Doronicum, Erigeron, Echinops, Gaillardia, Geum, Gypsophila, Helenium, Helleborus (the Christmas rose), Heuchera, Helianthus, Papaver nudicaule (Iceland Poppy), Pæony, Pyrethrum, Scabiosa caucasica, Solidago, Thalictrum, Trollius, and large numbers of Michaelmas Daisies.

Naturally some varieties are more suited than others to cut flower work. The fullest details of best varieties appear in my book *Cut Flowers for the Home*.

For the cut flower border the perennials will again be planted in rows 1 ft apart, but in the case of the taller kinds like delphiniums a space of 2-3 ft will be allowed in the rows, and the plants from row to row will be staggered. The great thing is to go on with the standardized scheme, as thus any of the sundries used for staking, covering, hoeing, etc., fit any bed perfectly.

With perennials it is important to keep the flower heads cut to prevent them seeding even if they are not required for the house and it is advisable not to leave the rows down for more than three years. With Chrysanthemum maximum it is not a bad plan to lift the plants up every other year. Pæonies, which hate disturbance, may be left down eight or nine years.

11 Roses and the Rose Garden

One can hardly imagine a garden in England without a rose bush or two. Most gardens have special beds set aside for roses and the large ones have definite Rose Gardens. There is never any need to extol the virtues of the rose, for it is as well known in the humblest of cottages as it is in mansions and palaces. The rose looks at its best when massed. It needs to be sheltered from winds and seems to prefer the heavier soils on the whole.

Beds of Roses.

There are roses to suit almost every condition. There are special varieties that do well even in smoky towns and cities; there are ramblers and climbers for walls and fences; there are types that are quite happy to be grown as hedges; there are species that look perfect in a shrub border; there are kinds which do well in the greenhouse. Roses look as well when cut in bowls in the house as they do massed in a rose bed.

Grouping the Roses

Roses may be divided into groups under various headings. There are :

The Standards. These have tall stems usually 3 ft 6 in. high, the budding being done on Rugosa.

Half Standards. These have stems 2 ft 6 in. high.

Polyantha Standards. Usually budded on stems 2 ft high.

Weeping Standards which have a stem similar to the Standard but the growths droop and trail on to the ground in an attractive manner. Because of this they are often budded on stems 4-5 ft 6 in. high.

The Hedge Roses which are usually planted in double rows, 18 in. apart; certain varieties being chosen as being specially suitable for the purpose.

Tea Roses. Usually denoted by a capital T. These seem to do better in France than in England, but when they do get established here they grow marvellously well.

Hybrid Perpetuals or H.P. Roses, which, despite their name, are never perpetually blooming! Very few of the varieties ever bloom in the autumn and thus most gardeners prefer the next class.

Hybrid Teas. Commonly called H.T.'s. This is a perpetually blooming rose, the blooms of which are long and pointed, whereas the roses of the H.P.'s are generally flat. You will always find 100 H.T.'s in gardens today to every H.P.

The Pernetianas or Pernets. This group was originally derived from a crossing made with the Austrian briars. The group has now become lost through inbreeding with the H.T.'s. It is the Pernets which have, through marriage, provided the glorious oranges and bronzes, etc.

The Wichurianas and Hybrid Wichurianas, often called W.'s and H.W.'s. This is the rambler rose group, which

ROSES

Hybrid Tea

Hybrid
Perpetual

Pernetiana

came to us through the lovely wild rose of Japan. The long shoots are pliable and easily trained. Some varieties are crosses between the Wichurianas and H.T.'s Most ramblers are Wichurianas but not all.

Multiflora Rambler or Climbing Polyantha, usually described as M.R., Crimson Rambler is a typical variety in this class, while in addition there are the Climbing Hybrid T's which are really sports of the varieties of the same name. There is for instance Madame Heriot, the H.T., and Climbing Madame Heriot, the C.H.T. Ramblers do not as a whole bloom more than once, but climbers do.

The Polyanthas. These are one of the latest additions to the family and are really crosses between the Rosa Multiflora and H.T.'s. There are also the hybrid polyanthas, usually called H. Poly, which are said to be nearer ever-blooming than any other type of rose.

The Bourbons. This is the good old-fashioned rose group closely related to the China types. It is very sweetly scented, and an autumn flowerer. My favourite is Souvenir de la Malmaison.

ROSES

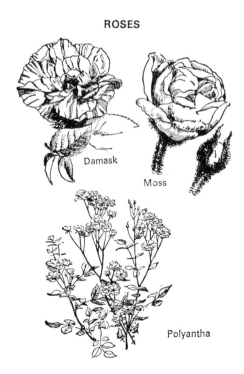

Damask

Moss

Polyantha

The Noisettes. A blend between the Tea, Musk and China Roses.

Then in addition there are the Moss Roses, the **Provence** (the old type of Cabbage Rose), and the Damask **Roses** which have now practically disappeared. They were originally used for making the famous scent Attar of Roses. There are always special species to study for those who **are** interested, like the Ayrshire Briars and the Cherokee Rose from China.

Soil Preparation. With proper cultivation and the correct use of organic manures, most soils can be made to grow good roses. Like other plants they dislike waterlogging and correct drainage must be ensured. In the case of very heavy badly drained soils it is not a bad plan to bury a mass **of** clinkers or old brickbats 18 in. to 2 ft down.

Fork the ground over shallowly, removing any roots **of** perennial weeds seen. Complete forking as early as possible so as to allow the soil to settle before planting the bushes. Organic fertilizers such as 'meat and bone' meal or **fish** manure should be worked into the top 2 in. at 3-4 oz **to** the sq. yard when the surface soil is being made level, ust prior to planting. In addition finely divided wood ashes, if available, at half a lb. per sq. yard. Further applications of such fertilizers may be given at intervals **of a fortnight** from the beginning of May until the beginning of June at one oz per sq. yard in each case on occasion.

With shallow soils it is a good plan to use roses grafted on to Rugosa stocks which because of their fibrous rooted propensities are more adapted to shallow land. Further dressings of well-rotted compost or sedge peat should be applied as top dressings in May to act as a mulch. Get the preparation done early. Planting really ought to take place by the end of November in heavy land, though up till the end of December in light land.

Planting. When the trees arrive give them a good drink. Put them into a bucket or tub of water. Never allow the roots to be exposed to drying winds. If they arrive during frosty weather do not unpack them but leave them in the straw bales till the frost is over. Always plant in the autumn, but should it be necessary to delay planting till March it is advisable to prune the trees before planting s in this way they get into growth more quickly. Cut the trees quite hard back, say to within four or five buds of the point at which the stock was budded.

Dig a hole, say 18 in. across, so as to be able to spread the roots out evenly from the centre. Plant so that the union of the stock and scion is just below soil level and no more. You can always find this union. It is usually above the soil mark on the stock. Never allow the roots to be doubled up against the side of the hole, and if there are some straggling roots that seem to go far beyond the circumference of the hole prepared for the bush, or tree, cut these back with a knife or sharp pair of secateurs.

Once the roots are in position at the bottom of the hole and spread out properly, put the soil back spadeful by spadeful, gently moving the rose up and down slightly so that the particles of soil may find their way in between the roots and get into immediate contact with them. Firm all the time with the foot as the spadefuls go in and do not be afraid of pressing down hard. Never plant in wet weather or when the soil is wet.

In very cold districts it may be advisable to give the bushes a little protection in the winter months. This applies particularly to the Pernetianas. Straw is usually used for the purpose, strewn over and around the bushes. It must be removed immediately the frost is over.

When planting climbers close to a wall or fence do not make the hole too close to the structure, or the roots will not get sufficient rain. The hole should be at least 1 ft away from the base of fences or walls. In the case of pergolas, it is better to plant the roses between the posts rather than actually against them.

Beds and Distance Apart. With bush roses the plan should be to get a good mass of roses and not be able to see the soil between. Plant the normal varieties 20 in. apart and the dwarfer kinds 18 in. apart. Always aim at having really large beds so as to obtain the best effect. The smallest bed that is worth while is one 4-4½ ft in diameter. This will hold seven Polyanthas. Those who want to plant seven Teas or Hybrid Teas will have to have a bed 5 ft in diameter.

Square and rectangular beds are easy to cope with. The front row of bushes will be 1 ft away from the pathway and the other rows 1 ft 8 in. away from each other. A convenient-size bed is 5½ ft wide and this takes 3 rows of

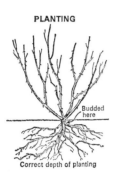

PLANTING

Budded
here

Correct depth of planting

bushes, the middle row of which should be planted alternately with the other rows and in such a manner that the bushes are not exactly opposite each other. It is possible in this way to have two extra bushes per bed.

The idea of covering the beds with sedge peat or compost one in. deep is to control all annual weeds and so make hoeing unnecessary. At the end of the year if the worms have pulled in a ¼ in. layer then another ¼ in. layer of sedge peat or compost must be applied so as to keep the mulch at a depth of one inch.

Manuring. Reference has already been made to this under the heading Soil Preparation, but undoubtedly, it is necessary to give an initial application of organic matter, preferably in May in the south and early in June in the colder parts of the north. Properly composted vegetable refuse should be applied all over the soil and the material acts as a mulch. In addition use a complete organic fertilizer like fish, 'meat and bone' meal, poultry manure or 'hoof and horn' meal at the rate of 3-4 oz per sq. yard each season, say in April. It is often necessary to give potash in addition in the case of light soils; finely divided wood ashes should be a applied at half a pound per sq. yard.

If especially large blooms are desired or where it is felt that the roses are not growing sufficiently strongly, liquid Marinure may be applied once a fortnight in June in accordance with the instructions given on the bottle. Fortnightly feedings are usually desirable and these may be repeated later on in August if a special crop of blooms is desired.

Routine Work. Towards the end of April it may be necessary with bush roses to do a certain amount of dis-shooting, the aim being to remove young growths that look as if they are going to overcrowd the centre of the tree. These can easily be pinched out with the thumb and forefinger. It is seldom necessary to rub out more than three or four shoots per bush.

Trace the sucker to it's point of origin and pull it off

If in April it is found that the top bud or buds of any growths that have been pruned back refuse to break, cut these shoots back further still to just above an upward growing eye that obviously is not blind or dead.

Keep the beds hoed regularly to prevent any weeds developing; hoeing should start in the spring and continue till the autumn.

Cut back well down the current growth to the strongest lateral

The placing of medium grade sedge peat or compost on the surface of the ground all over the beds is known as mulching. This is done for the purpose of (1) keeping the roots cool, (2) of controlling the weeds, (3) to control the disease black spot by preventing the spores blowing up from the soil, and (4) in order to supply organic matter to the ground.

To ensure large size blooms, disbud. At the ends of the young growths will usually be found one terminal bud and two or three side buds. The side flower buds are pinched out when quite young and this gives the terminal or central bud the whole of the manufactured food being pumped up into that shoot. This work is done with bush roses, principally with H.T's and does not apply to Polyanthas or other types.

With bush roses also, and to a certain extent with standards and half-standards, look out for suckers growing up from the stock. The suckers have quite a different appearance from the rest of the growth on the bushes or trees. The leaves are usually smaller and there are more thorns or spines. Often on the sucker these spines or thorns are smaller, darker and less hooked. Cut out the suckers immediately they are seen, at their point of origin from the roots. This will prevent them growing again.

Directly the blooms fade on bush roses and on standards and ramblers cut back the growths carrying the dead flowers. If this is done after the first blooming in June in the case of H.T's the second blooming usually takes place in September. Don't cut the growths back harder than 6 or 7 in. or you may encourage basal buds to break into growth and these will be killed by the frost during winter months.

Pinch out all but the strongest bud

In the spring and summer spray with Liquid Derris if necessary to kill insects. You cannot control a bad aphis attack with one spraying. Ladybirds however can. Diseases like Mildew and Black Spot may be controlled by spraying with Karathane and Captan.* Encourage ladybirds as these eat the aphides (as do the larvae of the ladybirds known as "niggers", they are like tiny little alligators!).

Though roses will withstand the long droughts, the disease called Mildew is particularly bad on plants that are

---

* Mulches of properly made compost contain antibiotics and as a result attacks of fungus diseases are rare.

suffering from lack of water. When watering has to be done it should be by the hose and an overhead whirling sprinkler. This should be left in position for at least half an hour at each spot so that a good wetting with artificial rain will be given.

In the autumn, rake up the prunings, fallen leaves, etc., and put them on the compost heap to rot down with other vegetable matter collected. Use an activator on the heap, and the heat engendered will kill the disease spores and insect eggs.

Go over the supports of standard rose, ramblers, etc., each winter and see that they are firm in the ground. Undo all ties, loosen strips of felt if necessary and re-tie afterwards. See that the tarred string is never allowed to cut into the bark.

Pruning. One of the most difficult things to do in a book is to explain pruning. You cannot, for instance, cover all types of roses in one paragraph. Generally speaking, however, rose pruning may be divided into two main operations. (1) The cutting back of shoots in order to produce strong growth the following season, and (2) The complete removal for obvious reasons, of dead wood, diseased wood, weak wood, misplaced and crossing or rubbing branches. When pruning to promote growth a cut is made just above a bud pointing outwards. When pruning for removal the growths are cut right away to the base.

Always prune with a sharp knife or pair of secateurs. People with tender hands often wear a pair of gardening gloves when doing the work. Keep the knife blade sharp by using the smooth hone. With old trees it is sometimes necessary to have a small saw. The cuts must be made cleanly for when jagged cuts are made they take longer to heal.

With bush roses most people believe in hard pruning and this consists of cutting back the current year's wood to within two or three eyes of its base the first year and to within six eyes of its base in subsequent years. Varieties that come under the heading H.P. are usually not pruned any harder than to within eight buds.

Detailed Pruning Instructions As the various types of roses have to be pruned differently I propose dealing with the various classes under separate headings.

H.P.'s, H.T.'s and Noisettes. Prune during March or early April, cutting out the dead wood and the diseased and weak shoots. Thin out the centre of the bush if necessary; cut back the well-ripened shoots of the previous year's growth to within four eyes of their base.

The dead wood may be cut away in late autumn.

Climbing Roses of the H.T. and H.P. Class. Prune in March, removing a sufficient number of growths over two years of age to prevent them from being too crowded. (Some prefer to do this after flowering in the summer and they then tie the new shoots in their place.) Prevent the base becoming bare by shortening back one or two of the older shoots every four years. Another method of dealing with this problem is to bend down one of the younger shoots to cover the bare parts. If it is necessary to cut back any side growths or laterals this should be done within three or four buds of their base.

Moss Roses. Remove the old wood and thin the bush out. Shorten the laterals from the two-year-old wood to within four eyes of their base. Cut back the vigorous young growth to within four buds early in March.

Pernetianas. These are very liable to frost damage because they are pithy. Always prune to make the cut below the frosted part which can easily be seen because the wood is dead. If the winter is mild prune as for H.T.'s.

Ramblers. Thin in the autumn, retaining the best first and second year old wood. Shorten one or two of the less strong stems to induce buds to break at the base. This shortening must not be done till the early spring. The main pruning can be done directly after flowering ceases.

RAMBLERS (Wichuraianas). Thin these out in the autumn and finish the pruning early in March. Each year they should send up from their base a number of strong shoots 10-15 ft long. Every year one or more of the oldest growths should be cut out in the autumn and any laterals on two-year-old stems should be cut back hard in the spring. The growths should then be spread out like a fan.

Where there is plenty of young wood, cut back all the old wood to its base and retain the new. Under this method you never get quite such a big plant. When a very large plant is required for festooning over a pergola, the younger growths should be used to furnish the lower parts of the pergola, and the older growths to beautify the more distant parts.

Standard Roses. Prune these in a similar manner as for H.T.'s or H.P.'s. In the case of special varieties like **W. H.** Richardson and Gloire de Dijon only remove the superfluous shoots and worn out growths, and shorten slightly. Never cut these back hard.

Weeping Standards. Shorten the growths that actually trail on the ground; remove the older shoots as near to the head as possible. If there are not many new shoots, leave some of the older growths in, but these seldom flower well. If there should be a super-abundance of young strong growths thin these out to prevent overcrowding.

Roses Pegged Down. Strong roses of the 'climber' type can be used for carpeting the soil. J. B. Clark, Karl Druschki and Zéphyrine Drouhin are typical varieties that can be used for this purpose. The longest and ripest shoots, about four per plant, are retained, cut to the length required and pegged down horizontally. The other growths are cut out completely. Do this work in March.

During the summer young shoots grow out from the base of the plants and the following March these shoots, which by then will have flowered, will be cut away and fresh growths will be trained in their place.

Monthly Pruning Guide

FEBRUARY. The Rugosas.

EARLY MARCH. Wichurianas, Ramblers, H.T.'s, H.P.'s, Polyanthas, Pernetianas, Climbing H.T.'s, Climbing H.P.'s, Climbing T.'s and Noisettes.

LATE MARCH. The Scotch and Sweet Briars.

APRIL. The Banksians.

JUNE AND JULY. Prune back roses that have flowered with a view to autumn flowering.

AUGUST AND SEPTEMBER. Prune ramblers immediately after flowering. Thin Wichuriana ramblers.

Roses for Cut Flowers

Those who want to cut roses for the house day by day should plant bushes 18 in. by 18 in. and prune hard each early April. Disbudding should be done as advised on page 121, and the bushes should be fed during the summer with Marinum once every fourteen days during flowering. About a quarter of a gallon diluted food should be given each time.

The following varieties are particularly useful for cut flower purposes : Lady Sylvia, a rose pink, scented; Baccara, a brilliant vermilion; Whisky Mac, a golden amber; Madame Butterfly, a salmon; McGredy's Yellow; Picture, a rose pink; Pink Parfait, rose pink, strong stems; Betty Uprichard, a coppery pink; Pascali, a disease resistant white; Golden Melody, a salmon flesh shaded with rose.

Always cut roses early in the morning and early in the bud stage. Cut with as long a stem as possible.

Different types of Roses

Reference has already been made in the early part of the chapter to the different types of roses it is possible to grow. It is now time to deal with these various roses under different headings and to mention one or two of the best varieties. It is impossible to do more than pick out my favourites in each connection.

Dwarf Polyanthas. This is a group of roses of dwarf habit all of which produce compact clusters of small flowers throughout the season. They are excellent for bedding and make grand edgings for borders. They can be had in a wide range of colouring and the foliage is usually disease-free. The Floribundas are more vigorous and require more room and I have used some of the stronger types for low hedges. Some of the varieties, for instance, Anne Poulsen, are fragrant.

My favourite Dwarf Polyanthas are Paul Crampel, an orange scarlet; Gwyneth, a clear yellow; Sheelagh Baird, pink and rich rose; Little Dorrit, a coral salmon; Ideal, a dark scarlet; Ellen Poulsen, a cherry rose; and Lady Reading, a crimson.

Floribundas. These are an attractive form of bedding roses with continuity of flowering. They are on the whole vigorous and should be planted 24 in. to 24 in.

The following are some of my favourites : Charles Dickens, a semi-double salmon; Dearest, a soft rosy salmon; Elizabeth of Glamis, salmon pink; Franklin Englemann, bright scarlet; Ice White, a scented white; Lilac Chain, pure mauve; Jiminy Cricket, scented orange salmon; Lili Marlene, crimson scarlet; Merlin, yellow, overlayed pink; Red Gold, a bicolour of red and gold; Sea Pearl, pearly pink, upright; Arthur Bell, a chrome yellow; Dicksons Flame, a flame scarlet; and Lively Lady, a vermilion double, fragrant.

Weeping Standards. It was Dean Hole who described weeping standards as a 'floral mountain', for the branches must be trained to an umbrella shape and grow with their long branches tumbling downwards. It is usual to have a hoop of wood or wire conveniently supported near the top of the tree, over which the growths are trained. The trees should be 5 or 6 ft in height to give plenty of room for the drooping branches.

You cannot expect a weeping standard to flower the first summer after planting, for it is necessary to cut back the growths to five eyes from the base. It is as a result of such pruning that strong weeping growths develop that flower the following year. Plant the weeping standards in October or early November while the soil is still warm. You will need to have them as single specimens on the lawn, or in the front garden. You cannot mix them in a rose bed or plant them in a shrub border.

Though weeping standards are expensive to buy they generally last for about twenty years so that they are good value for money.

My favourite varieties are : Albertine, a coppery pink; Lady Godiva, a flesh pink; Alberic Barbier, a creamy white; Emily Gray, a yellow; and Excelsis, a bright scarlet.

China Roses. These are very free-flowering and many claim that they are in bloom a month throughout the spring until late autumn. They are excellent for massing and for hedges. When pruning they are best thinned and one or two of the strongest shoots cut back to encourage new growths from the base. I usually do the thinning after the main summer flowering but some friends of mine cut theirs down hard late in April.

My favourite China roses are : Laurette Messimy, a rose-shaded yellow; Common China, a fragrant pink; Armoise Superiere, a crimson; Perle D'or, yellow shaded orange.

Moss Roses. These have received their name because on the outside of the buds there grows a moss-like calyx. They thus look particularly attractive. All moss roses are strong growers and must be pruned moderately in consequence. The old wood can be removed and the bush thinned out as described on page 124. Those who love fragrant roses should certainly go in for this type. My favourite moss roses are : Common Moss, a pale rose; Crested Moss, a heavily mossed pink; Golden Moss, a yellow; Blanche Morreau, a white; and Henryi Martin, a deep red.

Musk Roses. The musk roses are the most sweetly scented type of all. The actual aroma comes from the stamens. The musk roses planted today are largely hybrids and look well as isolated bushes or massed in beds. They make quite a good hedge. Prune them as little as possible. Just thin out some of the old wood in March. My favourite musks are : Cornelia, a strawberry flushed yellow; Penelope, a fine pink; Vanity, a bright pink; Bonn, an orange scarlet; Elmshorn, a reddish pink; Falicia, fragrant pink shaded yellow; Prosperity, a white.

Rugosas. These have rough leaves and thorns. They are hardy and free-flowering and usually produce large blooms the whole summer. They bear brilliant red seed pods in the autumn and so are very ornamental. They require little pruning after the first season except perhaps the cutting away of thin and dead wood. Rugosas are grand hedging plants. My favourite Rugosas : Blanc double de Coubert, a very fragrant white; F. J. Grootendoorst, a bright red; Cecile Brunner, a blush pink; Broomfield Abundance, similar to above; Pink Grootendoorst, a clear pink with frilled rosettes; Rose à Parfum de L'Hay, brilliant red; Scabrosa, deep mauve pink.

Provence Roses. An old hardy fragrant type of rose; a very gross feeder; one that loves plenty of organic manure. There is the old cabbage rose as it is usually called; the Red Provence, a deep rose with a large open flower; and White Provence, a pure white. The Provence roses are pruned in the same way as the Moss Roses. Common Provence is a fragrant pink.

Bourbons. These have smooth thick leaves, large curved thorns and the flowers are produced on laterals growing on the old wood, very little pruning is practised as a rule other than to thin out and cut back some of the laterals by about one-third.

My favourite Bourbons are : Zéphyrine Drouhin, a sweet scented silvery pink, very free flowering and grand for a hedge; and Kathleen Harrop, a pale sort of Zéphyrine.

Damasks. The roses that are said to have been introduced by the Crusaders; the flowers are fragrant, borne in clusters, and the leaves are apple-green. They are all of them sum-

Lupins

mer flowering. In March the shoots should be thinned out if necessary. The pruner should aim to keep the best one year old and two year old wood, as well as the strongest well-placed laterals.

Rose Species. There are a large number of botanical species which are usually planted in shrub borders. Some have brightly coloured fruits; others have attractive crimson foliage; some have red thorns; others are intensely scented. Some nurserymen specialize in these species and those who are interested in planting them should study the catalogues.

My favourite species are : Hugonis, a brilliant single yellow; Joseph's Coat, a yellow orange and carmine; Moyesii Geranium, a dwarf crimson lake; Rosa pomifera, because of its red apple-like fruits; Rosa willmottiae, because of its orange red fruits and fragrant foliage; Rosa moyesii, because of its ruby red flowers and sealing wax red pitcher-shaped fruits; and Rosa alba because it is the Jacobite Rose.

H.T.'s The bulk of the rose bushes planted today fall into this group, for the normal bush rose is undoubtedly the most popular of all.

The H.T.'s certainly furnish the finest most constant flowerers and best varieties both for exhibition and garden decoration. They dominate all others because of their exquisite colouring and graceful pleasing formation of the flowers. They are easy to prune.

There are such large numbers of varieties to choose from (and every year new introductions are made) that it is very difficult to do more than mention a few that have given good results in my garden, or that I have seen do particularly well in the gardens of friends, and clients.

Here then is a short list of good bedding sorts : Betty Uprichard, a salmon pink with carmine reverse; Blue Moon, a soft lilac; Fragrant Cloud, a coral red; Grandmere Jenny, yellow flushed pink; Josephine Bruce, a velvety crimson, scented; McGredy's Yellow, a primrose yellow; Mrs. Sam McGredy, a coppery orange scented; Papa Meilland, scented rich velvety crimson; Peace, a large yellow with a flush of pink; Speks Yellow, robust yellow; Super Star, bright vermilion; Wendy Cussons, deep cerise; Isabel Orty, deep pink with silvery reverse, fragrant; Paxali, a full white, long stems.

The following rambler roses may be considered as easy

to grow under most conditions: American Pillar, single rose pink, white eye; Albertine, reddish salmon beds, scented; Alberic Barbier, creamy white, shaded yellow; Crimson Shower, semi- double crimson; Emily Greig, yellow blooms with coppery foliage; Etain, sweet scented salmon pink; Minnehaha, a shell pink; Excelsa, a bright scarlet.

Recurrent Flowering Climbers. A newish type of climbing rose producing an abundance of colour. Altissimo, deep red flushed crimson, dark green foliage; Casino, a soft yellow; Coral Dawn, coral pink; Danse de Feu, orange red; Handel, deep carmine pink, ivory base; Pink Perpetué, double rich carmine pink; School Girl, a soft salmon; Swan Lake, a lovely white; and Mermaid, a sulphur yellow with glossy foliage (dislikes hard pruning).

Climbing Sports. These climbing roses are suitable for walls or pergola posts. They only require moderate pruning. They like overhead spraying with clean water on hot summer days. Climbing Allgold, a yellow; Climbing Ena Harkness, a scented crimson scarlet; Climbing Iceberg, a pure white; Climbing Orangeade, a lovely orange; Climbing The Doctor, a bright pink; Climbing Crimson Glory, a scented crimson; and Climbing Masquerade, a yellow, pink and scarlet.

Roses for the Town Garden

Those who live in towns and cities will be well advised not to grow T.'s, for they are useless in smokey areas. Even the more moderate growing Hybrid T.'s suffer badly as do the Pernetianas. As smokiness usually brings about soil acidity the rose bed should certainly be given dressings of hydrated lime, say at 4-5 oz to the sq. yard each year.

These roses should never be grown too close to walls or fences or even near to dense hedges. It is always important in a town garden to have the rose beds in a spot where there there is (1) good circulation of air, and (2) plenty of sunshine.

Don't grow varieties that are very susceptible to Mildew. Don't grow the delicate shades, cream, lemon or ivory. Do syringe the bushes over at least once a week in the evening, using clean water, preferably rain water. This keeps the leaves free from smuts.

The following varieties do well under town and city conditions both in the north and south:

Hybrid Musks – Penelope, Bonn.

Dwarf Polyanthas – all.

Rugosas – Grootendoorst, Scabrosa.

Hybrid Wichurianas (Climbers) – Excelsa, Chaplain's Pink, Easlea's Golden Rambler, Emily Gray.

Climbing Sports – Crimson Glory; The Doctor.

Hybrid Bourbons – Zéphyrine Drouhin, Kathleen Harrop.

H.T.'s – Fragrant Cloud, Mrs. Sam McGredy, Peace, Super Star, Josephine Bruce, Ernest H. Morse, Colour Wonder, Mischief, and Wendy Cursons.

Climbers for Walls

Ramblers are not really suited for training against walls because (1) they cannot stand the great heat given off by walls in the summer, and (2) they have to be cut down each year, and so it means a tremendous amount of cutting out of old wood and tying in of new – which is a nuisance.

Plant any of the following climbers which will give little trouble and which will spread themselves over the wall concerned quite quickly.

Climbing Allgold, a yellow; Climbing Madame Butterfly, a pink, apricot and gold; Climbing Edouard Heriot, a coral red; Climbing Etoile d'Hollande, a dark crimson; Climbing Ena Harkness, a crimson; and Climbing Iceberg, a white.

12 Flowering Shrubs in the Flower Garden

One of the simplest ways of getting a beautiful effect is by the use of the flowering shrub. In the long run it is one of the cheapest ways also, for the flowering shrub border will be down for years, and needs comparatively little looking after. If I were asked for the definition of a shrub I think I should call it a woody plant that doesn't form a single clean trunk. A tree has a single clean trunk but a shrub does not. Some shrubs, however, like the holly, will grow into trees if they are given the chance. Too often the beginner only thinks of evergreen shrubs and so the shrub border becomes dark, dull and unattractive. Many of the Victorian gardens and many of our town gardens now have shrub borders of this kind.

The heather garden at Arkley Manor.

In this chapter I concentrate on those shrubs which will make the garden more pleasant by their colour and form. In some cases it will be the flowers themselves. In other cases the colour of the bark in the winter, and yet in others the autumn tints of the foliage, or the beautiful colours of the fruits or berries. It is possible to have colour in a shrub border almost all the year round, as I will show.

It is as well to study the likes and dislikes of certain shrubs because to ignore completely some definite preferences is to court failure. For instance, the heathers and heaths hate lime and will not grow on chalky land. The rock roses and brooms insist on being in full sunshine. The rhododendrons and azaleas dislike lime and do best with some protection from full sunshine. On the whole, shrubs

METHOD OF WATERING
WALL SHRUBS

A drain-pipe is sunk into the
ground and filled with water
daily

will grow in almost any ground, providing it has been well worked.

Wherever shrubs are to be planted, the ground may be shallowly forked and good compost incorporated at the same time. A shrub border will be down for years and it is well worth while spending time preparing it. Do the very shallow forking a month or two before planting, to allow the ground to settle, and when planting make sure that the shrubs are in firmly. After planting and firming level, cover the bed with a one inch thick layer of powdery compost or medium grade sedge peat. This will prevent the annual weeds from growing and will provide a mulch which will conserve the moisture.

The great difficulty in planting shrubs is that they are usually obtained when small, and if they are put in at their correct distance apart, the shrub border has a very bare look about it for the first four or five years. It is necessary therefore to adopt one of two customs : (1) To plant up the border twice or three times as thickly as necessary and then dig out the shrubs in excess at the end of the four-year period. Or (2) To use the spaces between the small shrubs for growing annuals or biennials – the better of the two methods, on the whole.

If the border is to be planted up thickly, it is possible to dig up and transplant the shrubs not required to another part of the garden years later. This should be done just after the leaves fall in the autumn while the soil is still warm, though it is possible to do it during any period when the weather is open in the winter. Evergreen shrubs are best transplanted before activity ceases in the early autumn or activity has started in the late spring. When hollies, for instance, are transplanted in mid winter, they invariably die, yet shrubs obtained from some of our best nurseries, with a large ball of earth at their roots, will transplant quite successfully almost any time in the winter months.

Always dig the shrubs up with as big a root system as possible and with as great a ball of soil as possible, commensurate with carrying or wheeling the shrub from one part of the garden to another. See that the hole intended for their reception is large enough to enable the roots to be spread out evenly to their full extent. When covering up, fine soil should be worked in among the finer roots and all soil immediately in contact with the root system should be

trodden firmly. Try to plant at the same depth as the shrub
was growing previously. Shrubs have a habit of dying if
they are planted too deeply !

Tasteful Planting.   Take as much trouble and thought with
the arrangement of a flowering shrub border as with a
herbaceous border (see pages 133-43). Remember that the
shrubs are going to grow to a good height after a time, and
because many of them or so large, there will not be room
in a small garden for groups of a particular variety. One
large shrub will take the place of a group. Arrange the
shrub border so that the colour extends over as long a
period as possible. See that the dwarfer shrubs are to the
front and the taller ones to the back and aim at having an
even distribution of colour right along the border if possible. Keep in your mind's eye the needs of the different
shrubs, the ones that will appreciate a little shade, and the
others that insist on the full sunshine. Plan the colour
effects in such a manner that they do not clash one with
another.

BUDDLEIA

B. globosa

B. alternifolia

B. variabilis

Hints on Shrub Pruning

There is a mistaken belief in some quarters that all shrubs must be pruned at one period of the year or another. This is entirely untrue. Shrubs may be grown without any pruning at all, especially in gardens where there is plenty of room. On the other hand, there is need in nearly all cases to cut out dead wood, to remove crossing branches, to remove branches that are rubbing one another, and to cut out weak wood. Such pruning has been described as a 'sanitary operation', i.e. the removal of the diseased and dead wood prevents further infection, and the cutting out of the crossing branches lets in more light and air and so helps to ensure better ripened wood and in consequence more beautiful blossoms and berries.

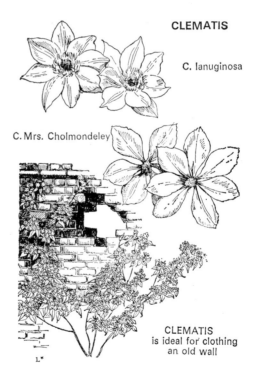

CLEMATIS

C. lanuginosa

C. Mrs. Cholmondeley

CLEMATIS
is ideal for clothing
an old wall

In smaller gardens there is need as a rule to carry out a certain amount of pruning each season to prevent shrubs overgrowing the space which has been allowed for them. Naturally this general shortening back of the branches encourages the production of new wood in its place, and in many cases this wood will be particularly floriferous. Much of the pruning in the normal way may be done in the winter. Then it is possible to cut out a large branch to a point just above a younger and smaller one which can be left growing in approximately the same direction, and by making the cut just above the lower branch, it can be ensured that there is no dead end or snag of wood left which will die back and may cause the entry of disease.

On the whole it is better to aim at pruning soon after flowering takes place. This allows the new growths to develop and to be ready for flowering the following season at the right time of the year. The shrubs which flower on the wood made the previous year there, must always be pruned as soon after flowering as possible, for this is the only way of allowing sufficient time for the shrub to produce its blossom buds for the following year. The shrubs which flower on the new or unripened wood produced that very season are generally pruned in the spring, rather than immediately after flowering, for if the pruning is done too early, new growths tend to be made immediately and these may be too soft for a hard winter, and so be killed.

Nellie Moser: a lovely clematis.

Putting it another way, it can be said that the shrubs that flower from June onwards on the current season's growth should be pruned back in the winter, while the shrubs which flower in the spring or early summer on the growths made the previous year should be pruned in the summer immediately after flowering. This group is the one into which the majority of the hardy shrubs fall. It is largely for this reason that the only pruning most gardeners do to them is the thinning out already described at the beginning of this pruning section and this need never be an annual operation.

It is customary to treat certain shrubs rather differently. For instance, the buddleia generally has all its young shoots shortened close back to the main stem early each season with the result that it produces long pendulous growths which bear the best blooms in the summer. The cutting back is aimed at producing very vigorous young growths. That lovely spiræa Anthony Waterer, for instance, gives a wonderful show when the shrub is cut back almost to the ground in the early spring. Hydrangea paniculata should be treated in a similar manner and so should Spiræa japonica.

Some shrubs are grown for the beautiful winter colours on the stems. These are usually pruned before the sap starts to rise in the spring, almost to ground level, and thus long, strong growths are produced during the season which give the yellow or red winter colour to the border. The Dogwoods and Willows are typical examples of this type of shrub.

Learn to appreciate first of all the normal size of the shrub concerned, then its habit of growth and lastly whether it is a slow or quick grower. These three things will help to give you the clue to the pruning that is desirable. The slow growers for instance, need very little attention at all; the quick growers may need regular attention especially after they have grown a good size. The heaths do not like being cut back when they are old and yet are apt to get a little leggy and so the dwarf plants often need pruning in the young stages to keep them stocky. The lovely Magnolia, on the other hand, which makes a large shrub,

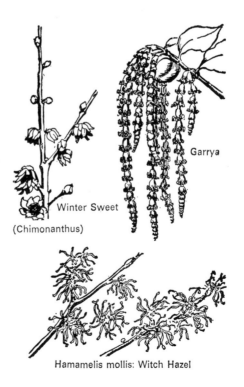

Garrya

Winter Sweet
(Chimonanthus)

Hamamelis mollis: Witch Hazel

hates being pruned at all, and must be allowed to develop at will.

Use a very sharp knife when pruning or a first-class pair of secateurs. If any really large cuts have to be made with the saw, these should be pared over afterwards with the knife, to leave the wounds smooth, and then a painting should be given with a thick white lead paint.

List of 'Easy-to Grow' Flowering Shrubs

It is impossible to give a complete list of all the hundreds of shrubs that might be grown in a garden. The beginner should study the descriptive catalogues of the best nurserymen for further advice. To guide readers, here is a list of shrubs which I have found amenable to the normal cultivation of gardens in almost all parts of the country. The kinds and varieties mentioned will give satisfaction and will prove a splendid introduction to any flowering shrub border of the future.

Lists of Flowering Shrubs
in their approximate flowering periods.

December-January
Chimonanthus fragrans
Erica carnea
Erica darleyensis
Garrya elliptica
Hamamelis mollis
Viburnum tinus

February-March
Azara microphylla
Berberis aquifolium
Berberis japonica
Cornus mas
Corylopsis spicata
Corylopsis veitchiana
Cydonia japonica & vars.
Daphne mezereum
Erica arborea
Erica lusitanica
Erica mediteranea
Forsythia intermedia
Forsythia suspensa
Hamamelis japonica
Hamamelis varnalis
Prunus spinosa
Prunus uniflora
Ribes laurifolium
Viburnum fragans
Viburnum grandiflorum

April-May
Azalea
Berberis darwinii
Berberis stenophylla
Cercis siliquastrum
Choisya ternata
Prunus triloba plena
Rhododendron
Ribes sanguineum
Rosemary
Spiræa arguta

Cytisus (Broom) hybrids
Daphne cneorum (6" high)
Jasminum officinale
Kerria japonica
Lilac (Syringa)

Spiræa confusa
Spiræa thunbergii
Spiræa Van Houttei
Tamarix tetrandra
Viburnum carlesii

June-July-August

Buddleia variabilis
Buddleia globosa
Ceanothus vars.
Colutea arborescens
Deutzia
Diervilla (Weigela)
Erica cinerea
Erica tetralix
Erica vagans
Escallonia macrantha
Genista virgata
Hydrangea hortensis
Lavender

Olearia haastii
Philadelphus (Mock Orange)
Santolina
Senecio greyii (grown for its
 leaves)
Spartium junceum
Spiræa aitchisonii
Spiræa japonica vars.
Tamarix petandra
Ulex gallii
Veronica vars.
Viburnum opulus

September-October

Abelia vars.
Caryopteris mastacanthus
Caryopteris tangutica
Daphne mezereum grandi-
 flora

Escallonia floribunda
Fatsia japonica
Hibiscus syriacus
Hydrangea paniculata
Phlomis fructicosa

November

Arbutus hybrida
Arbutus unedo & vars.
Eleagnus macrophylla
Elæagnus pungens

Jasminum nudiflorum
Lonicera fragrantissima
Lonicera standishii
Vinca difformis

My Favourite Flowering Shrubs.

Buddleia alternifolia
Ceanothus Gloire de
 Versailles
Cotoneaster salicifolia
 floccosa
Cytisus kewensis
Escallonia langleyensis
Forsythia intermedia
Abelia grandiflora

Hamamelis mollis
Magnolia stellata
Philadelphus Bouquet Blanc
Prunus triloba
Syringa Souvenir de Louis
 Spath
Viburnum carlesii

Garrya elliptica

Some of my Favourite Evergreeen Shrubs.

Berberis darwinii   Lavender

Berberis stenophylla   Osmanthus aquifolium

Choisya ternata   Phillyrea decora

Daphne neapolitana   Rhododendrons

Fatsia japonica   Rosemary

13 The Rock Garden

'What is a rock garden?' People certainly have different ideas – some of them rather odd. Again and again I find that house owners have made a heap of soil say, in a shady part of the garden; have covered it with brickbats, old stones, pieces of marble and the like; and then have planted up this peculiar 'excrescence' with ferns, perrywinkle, an odd primrose or two, a couple of aubretia, and perhaps some Chinese lanterns and then have taken me down the garden to show me this 'atrocity' with pride.

A rock garden should be made naturally. It should be constructed with care and with the right environment. As invariably the root system of the rock or alpine plant is eight or nine times greater than the part above ground there must be a good body of soil below. Other plants will exist on the ledge of a rock in almost no soil at all; they are the kinds of plants that absorb the bulk of their nourishment from the atmosphere. Yet other plants grow in pockets that are made up of well-rotted vegetable refuse mixed with particles of flakes of stone or rock. Others grow in a position where they are completely sheltered from winds. The good rock garden will provide all kinds of positions and conditions in which the different types of plants will grow.

No rock garden should be made up of root stumps, bricks, and clinkers. It should be constructed of good weathered rock, preferably indigenous to the district. These rocks should be laid in position so that they look natural. A rock garden can give a sense of height, depth and distance, if the rocks are carefully placed. Its original cost may appear to be high but if this capital cost is spread over a period of years, it will be found to be cheap as compared with other forms of gardening.

Remember that the rock garden is being made to accommodate plants that like growing under particular conditions. The very words 'alpine plants' give the secret of the situation. Here are plants that come from the Swiss Alps or from the mountains of China or Peru which grow where they are covered with snow throughout the winter and then in the summer the sun beats down on them. They are used to having ice-cold water at their roots, and though they are covered with snow in winter the cold is dry and so they live through the frosty weather. So often they hate our moist winters and have to be protected.

The good rock garden enables the gardener to have a large number of different kinds of dwarf plants in a comparatively small area, and when a rock garden is carefully planned it not only looks bright in the spring, but it can be very colourful at other periods of the year. If it is planned in such a way that it is slightly raised, or at any rate certain parts of it, the hoeing and titivation can be done without continual bending. Very often, too, because Alpines like growing in barren soil, weeds do not flourish.

The Position   Have your rock garden in a sunny place, for even if there are some Alpines that prefer shade, the big rocks you will use will certainly provide such spots. Never have the rock garden under trees where there will be a perpetual drip of moisture from the branches. Choose a high level if possible, but if a low spot has to be chosen see that the whole area is perfectly drained. When making a rock garden in a town where the area is small, make a mound of soil, with varying contours, on the south side with a path skirting its irregularly shaped outline. It is always a good thing to make the rock garden a separate feature where possible and to have a narrow bed of flowering shrubs for instance used as a division.

The Stone. As has already been suggested it is a very good plan to use the natural stone of the district. Those in Kent can use the Kentish Rag; those in Surrey and Sussex, the typical sandstone; those in Devon and Cornwall and parts of Wales, the harder stones like granite (though these are never so good); those in Somerset the weather-worn limestone or those in Derbyshire or Cumberland, that very attractive limestone that is both water- and weather-worn. Where there is no particular 'county stone', imported rocks are used with great effect. There are many rock gardens of Derbyshire limestone, for instance, all over the country.

If you can use local stone, the work is considerably cheaper. Remember when buying stones that three-quarters of the bulk of each one of them will never be seen and they should have quite a massive appearance before being laid into position. I have known, in big gardens, for there to be two or three stones that weigh half a ton or more each and all the remainder to weigh three cwts. each; even for quite small rock gardens the two or three main stones should weigh 5 cwts., and the others, say, 1 cwt. each. I mention these facts because I want to emphasize the need for using good rocks, and not little stones.

Using the Rocks Intelligently. It is not necessary to start with a mound or sloping soil because the lower stones, when placed in position, may give some hint of a need for further height, so soil may have to be brought to that point. You must start bedding in the rocks at the lowest point and build upwards. They must be laid in position so that they look like a natural outcrop. They should be given a slight backward slope so that the rain gets down to the roots of the plant; then as further rocks are put in position, they will remain at the same 'tilt'. The general slope of the strata should then be followed right through so that the whole thing looks natural.

Look at the face of the stone to be exposed and see if it is covered with any particular markings. Look for what we gardeners call graining and the weather markings. Watch for colours and try to blend all these into one whole. Sometimes there are vertical marks produced by rain and frost which may soon determine whether the stone is in its right position or not. In limestone rocks there are invariably horizontal lines which show the strata, and how much better it is to use rocks that have been weathered rather than those that have been quarried straight out of the bowels of the earth.

Ram soil tightly at the back of the rocks to keep them in position. See that pockets are provided and in some cases quite large areas for the plants you are going to grow. When rocks are to be placed one above the other, separate them by using hard stones as if they were 'pit props'. By keeping one large boulder a few inches off the other it prevents the soil that should be between them from getting squashed. See that the upper rock stands from the lower one and does not completely overlap or overhang it. Above all, make the rock garden look natural. Don't have the stone sticking out higgledy-piggledy anywhere.

Do not make the mistake of trying to get tremendous elevations and deep depressions into a space of 20 sq. yards. You only need slight undulations and a gentle slope. Don't make the mistake either of not being able to get at your plants. Make it possible when building, to gain easy access to every part of the rock garden for purposes of weeding or giving other attention to plants. Always remember the

Asters

Bartonia aurea

Carnation 'Chabeaud Giant'

Dahlia 'Collarette'

root run. This must be the first consideration. There must not be stagnant moisture below. Rank animal manure must not be used.

A spot must be provided for the lime haters where a special compost can be used consisting of two parts of acid soil, one part of peat and one part of silver sand, to which can be added a good helping of granite chippings. When other pockets have to be made up, these may consist of six parts of good soil, one part good horticultural peat, one part of rough silver sand, one part of limestone chippings and one eighth part mortar rubble if available and if not, ground limestone. In the case of primulas and gentian it is better to use six of peat and one of soil and no lime.

General Remarks When planting up the rock garden, tend to use large drifts and eschew tiny patches. Many species, for instance the Gentians, like to grow close together and so have their roots intermingled. Give the vigorous growers plenty of room or otherwise they will smother plants near them. Prolong the flowering season of any particular part of the rock garden by arranging for late types of plants to be interplanted with the early flowering kinds. It is quite a good idea to plant bulbs among the later flowering species, for the foliage and flowers of the bulbs will grow through their carpeting friends quite happily.

Always choose the best aspect for each type of plant. Never cramp the roots and if you buy pot plants see that you spread the root systems out after knocking the plants out of their pots – before you actually set them in the ground. Keep the carpeters towards the front of the rock garden on the whole and the taller plants to the back. Be prepared to water in May, should it be dry, and give protection from east winds if necessary by putting up a temporary sacking or hurdle screen. This is especially necessary during the first year after planting.

Once the rock garden has been established, each year in the spring all the pockets may be given a light top dressing of compost, i.e. the same type of soil mixture as used originally in that particular pocket or drift. Any rocks that may have been loosened by the frost should be made firm. Hand weed to prevent seeding; a 3-pronged carving fork is useful for the purpose. Control slugs by putting little heaps of blue Draza pellets every 3 ft or so if necessary or distribute them evenly over the area.

Keep weeding in the summer and stir the surface of the soil with the hand fork if there is no compost or sedge peat mulch on the soil. Remove the heads of plants as they go out of flower to prevent them seeding. Cut back the straggling plants after flowering, if necessary, by half. Certain of the older plants may need dividing and replanting.

In the autumn it may be necessary after a few years to renew some of the old pockets and supply new compost. Cut back the dead growth and remove any leaves from trees that may have fallen on to the rock garden. Protect the woolly-leaved plants with sheets of glass held in position over them by clips. There are special fixtures for the purpose. The glass should be 5 or 6 in. above the plants. This gives them all the protection they require.

Plants to Grow
There are hundreds of rock garden plants that might be grown. All that can be done here is to attempt to divide the plants up into various groups and make mention of just a few which I have found to be easy to grow or particularly attractive. The reader can increase his knowledge by going to good shows, by studying the garden press, by looking at the catalogues of well-known firms and of course by personal experience.

Spreaders and Ramblers. The plants that come into this group are easy to grow and are not fastidious as to soil or position. They can be planted any time in the early autumn, or from March to May. They like an open situation but they will put up with partial shade.

ACHILLEA UMBELLATA. Silvery leaves, white flowers in June, 6 in. high.

AJUGA REPTANS PUPUREA. Purplish leaves and blue flowers in May and June, 6 in. high.

ALYSSUM SAXATILE COMPACTUM. Greyish green leaves, yellow flowers from March-May, 9 in. high.

AUBRIETIA. Numerous varieties, varying in colour, pink, red, mauve, purple. April-June, 4-6 in high.

CAMPANULA ROTUNDIFOLIA. Small green leaves, numerous blue-bell shaped flowers. June and July, 9 in.

DIANTHUS DELTOIDES. Spiky leaves and small rose-pink flowers June-August. 12 in.

ERODIUM. Many kinds which have geranium-like

flowers followed by seed pods which look like birds' beaks.

HELIANTHEMUM. Many varieties of rock roses which flower from June-July, in varied shades of yellow, orange, pink and red. Like hot dry positions.

IBERIS SEMPERVIRENS. An evergreen candytuft bearing masses of pure white flowers from June-August, 9 in. high.

OXALIS. Most of the plants spread rapidly and flower from March-October. Floribunda has pink flowers; corniculata has orange flowers.

SAXIFRAGA. Many different types, some with red, some with white flowers. They form dense tufts of soft green foliage and produce either white or red flowers according to variety, some from May-June and others in April and May.

SEDUM. The stonecrop family, which have small thick succulent leaves and starry flowers.

VERONICA SAXATILIS. Bears rich blue flowers with crimson eye and has trailing stems. Flowers from June-September, grows 3 in high.

VIOLA CORNUTA. Bears bluish purple flowers from May-October on stems 6-9 in. high. There is a white variety.

The Bulbs and Tubers. There are a number of baby bulbs and tubers that look well in the rock garden. The autumn and winter flowering kinds should be planted in August but September or October is soon enough for those that bloom in the spring. Those that grow about 1 ft high should be planted 3-6 in. deep and 4-8 in. apart. The remainder should go in 1½-4 in. deep and 1-3 in. apart according to the size of the bulb. (The larger the deeper.) They all of them like a open situation and plenty of sun with the exception of the Trillium which prefers partial shade. Most of them can be left down for years – the tulips perhaps benefit by being lifted each alternate year.

Bulbs and Tubers to Grow.

ALLIUMS. Onion-like plants with narrow leaves and small heads of flowers bloom from June till July. 12-18 in. tall.

ANEMONES. Special rock garden kinds like Blanda which flowers from January until March and bears blue or pink flowers; 6 in. high.

CYCLAMENS. The dwarf species like Africanum which flowers in the autumn, a bluish lilac with 4-6 in. stems, or Coum, a rosy red which flowers from February till March on 4 in. stems.

ERANTHIS. The cheery little winter aconite which has bright yellow flowers like those of a buttercup. Hyemalis, in flower from January-March and only grows 3 in. tall.

ERYTHRONIUMS. Dog's tooth violet, bears flowers something like those of a cyclamen from April-May.

FRITILLARIAS bear well-shaped flowers beautifully marked with fine lines. Citrina is a pale yellow which flowers in May on stems 8-9 in. high.

IRISES. There are many dwarf bulbous sorts that are very suitable, like Alata which flowers in January and Reticulata a sweet-scented violet-purple which is at its best in February.

NARCISSUS. There are many babies in this daffodil family. The Hooped Petticoat narcissus is at its best in April and prefers a moist situation. It is only 6 in. tall. The cyclamen-flowered daffodil is the same height and is in bloom in February and March. Minimus is the smallest of all trumpet-daffodils only 3 in. tall, at its best in February. Angel's Tears is a small creamy white narcussus, which flowers in March. It is 6 in. tall.

TRILLIUM grandiflorum bears white flowers in April and May in three. 6-12 in. high.

TULIPS. There are many of the tulip species suitable for the rock garden, Greigii for instance is a vermilion scarlet which grows about 1 ft tall and is at its best in May. Kaufmanniana is a creamy white with a golden base plus a dull broad strawberry stripe outside. Grows 8 in. high.

Compact Plants. A large number of compact alpines do not spread and can be left undisturbed for years. September is the usual planting month though it is possible to get going in the early spring. They like a general soil mixture and, on the whole, not too rich. The hardy orchids enjoy shade or partial shade.

ÆTHIONEMA GRANDIFLORUM. Looks like a delicate candytuft, bushy in habit. Rose pink, likes lime, flowers April-July. 10 in. tall.

ANDROSACE. The rock jasmine. These are some of the choicest alpines. They love a moist well-drained root run and must be protected from rain in winter.

AQUILEGIA. The rock garden columbines are very dainty and are in flower from May-July.

ASTER ALPINUS. This is the baby Michaelmas Daisy, in flower from May-July bearing lilac-purple daisy-like blooms.

CAMPANULAS. Numbers of baby campanulas which make neat little plants. Some like Pulla only grow 3 in. high and others like G. F. Wilson are 9 in. tall. In flower from July-August.

CYPRIPEDIUMS. There are a number of baby Lady Slipper Orchids that grow only 9 or 10 in. tall and flower from May-June. They like semi-shade and moist peaty soil.

DIANTHUS. There are quite a family of alpine pinks whose flowers are sweetly scented from May-July.

ERIGERONS. Several species are suitable for the rock garden. The dwarf plants have marguerite-like flowers, Alpinus from June-August and Aurantiacus from May-June.

GENTIANS. The Gentians are very popular plants and the majority have lovely blue flowers. Acaulis is in flower from February to June; Freyniana from July-September, and Verna from April-June. All the gentians need understanding.

GERANIUMS. There are several dwarf species of these Cranesbills suitable for the rock garden. Most of them flower from June till September.

INULA ENSIFOLIA. A neat plant with small leaves and yellow daisy-like flowers. Grows 9 in. high, flowers from July-September.

LITHOSPERMUMS. Heavenly blue is probably the best variety. It quite likes lime and produces a mass of blue flowers from June -October, 9 in. high.

ŒNOTHERA MACROCARPA grows 6 in. high. Bears yellow flowers with large ornamental seed pods. At is best from June-September.

ORCHIDS. There are two or three which are quite suitable, latifolia, for instance is in flower in May, with purple flowers and dark spots, and maculata in May and June.

POTENTILLA TONGUEI bears orange buttercup-like flowers with a crimson centre, May-October, 4-6 in. high.

PRIMULAS. There are a large number of primulas that

on the whole prefer semi-shade and cool soil. Some like Juliae are only 4 in. tall and bear rose-purple flowers; others like Sikkimensis bear drooping heads of fragrant sulphur yellow flowers on stems 18 in. high from May-July.

SAXIFRAGES. There are compact species of saxifrages that belong mainly to the Kabschia and Encrusted sections. The leaves form neat greyish rosettes. Salmoni, dwarf, bears large white flowers. Irbing is a tiny flowered hybrid 3 in. high. Hosteii is 9-12 in. tall, and bears white flowers on red stems.

SEMPERVIVUMS. The house-leek family, the plants of which are grown more for their leaves than their flowers. They rather like old mortar rubble in the soil. As a group they flower in April-July.

VERONICA (syn. Hebe). There are one or two neat shrubby veronicas like Allioni which only grows 3-4 in. high and bears deep blue flowers in June and July.

ZAUSCHNERIA CALIFORNICA. Commonly called the Californian fuchsia, flowers from August-October. Bears brilliant scarlet flowers on stems 1 ft high.

Baby Shrubs

There are a number of baby shrubs that can be used with discretion in a rock garden to provide height and help to provide a sense of distance. There are several dwarf conifers that are very attractive. Some shrubs are grown for their berries and winter colouring; others for their flowers. The deciduous shrubs should be planted in the autumn and the evergreen kinds in April or September.

Varieties to Grow

CASSIOPE TETRAGONA. Bears tiny bell-like flowers tinged with pink. May not grow taller than 6 in.; flowers from March-June. Likes peat.

DAPHNE BLAGAYANA. A dwarf evergreen bearing creamy white fragrant flowers from March to April. Likes partial shade.

ERICAS. There are a number of baby heaths that do well in the rock garden. Most of them will not tolerate lime. By the careful choice of varieties it is possible to ensure flowering from January to December.

GAULTHERIA PROCUMBENS. Only grows 6 in. high; the flowers are white, followed by brilliant scarlet berries. Likes partial shade and peat.

GENISTA HISPANICA. An 18-in. shrub which forms a mound of bright yellow flowers. At its best in May and June.

JUNIPERUS. A number of compact shrubs with bluish-silver foliage. Most are pyramidal but there is a prostrate variety. The best types of conifer for the rock garden.

RHODODENDRONS. The baby alpine type bears numer-tubular flowers. Ferrugineum does not object to lime and bears pink blooms from April to June. Racemosum tolerates lime and bears white and rose pink flowers.

VERONICA (syn. Hebe). There are a number of baby types. Carnosula is an evergreen species with white flowers in the summer. Pimelioides has glaucous blue-grey leaves and purple flowers. It only grows 1 ft high.

Baby Roses

There are a number of delightful miniature roses quite suitable for the rock garden. They like an open position and any ordinary good soil.

New types of roses have been introduced which look well in the rock garden. I refer to Baby Darling, a salmon orange, 6 in. high; Cinderella, a white blush pink, 8 in.; Coralin, a red shaded orange, 8 in.; Easter Morning, a white, 12 in.; Little Flirt, red with yellow reverse, 12 in.; Pink Heath, rose pink, scented, 9 in.; Purple Elf, purple blue, 9 in.; Rosina, bright yellow, dark green leaves, 10 in.; Simple Simon, carmine red, 6 in.

14 Special Flower Borders

It is possible to have flower borders especially devoted to one particular family – an extension of the principle of the rose garden. There is no reason at all why you should not have a delphinium garden for instance, with borders and beds entirely devoted to the different kinds and varieties there are, but delphiniums by and large, are grown in the herbaceous border, and I only know of one garden which has borders devoted entirely to them. You see, it means that these particular borders are unbalanced. They are a mass of very tall plants with the result that you cannot see them all properly. They are ablaze for two or three weeks of the year and after that they are dull and dismal. There are, however, a number of what might be called 'specialist flowers' that are grown by themselves, and I propose in this chapter to deal with the most popular of them.

The Iris Garden It is often alleged that the Iris flowering period is too short but though few people realize it, it is quite possible to have irises blooming in the open for six months of the year. *Iris*

DIVIDING IRIS RHIZOMES

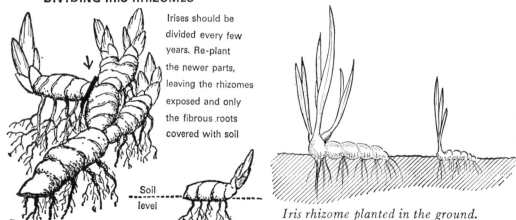

Irises should be divided every few years. Re-plant the newer parts, leaving the rhizomes exposed and only the fibrous roots covered with soil

Soil level

D

Iris rhizome planted in the ground.

stylosa for instance if planted in a warm sheltered spot, will be flowering gaily during December and January. Irises can be divided into the Bearded and Beardless types or as the real gardeners call them The Pogon and Apogon types; Pogon being from the Greek word meaning Beard.

If you are going to make an iris border, remember that the bulk of irises love sun and also insist on good drainage. They like to be planted at the correct season and they insist on good cultivation. On the whole the bearded irises do not like too much lime, though they often do quite well in areas known to be chalky. Their rhizomes or thick root stocks must be exposed so that the sun can warm them. When planting them they should never be put completely below the surface of the ground. They like to be fed regularly with an organic fertilizer like fish manure or meat and bone meal, at 3-4 oz to the sq. yard. Apply this in between and among the rhizomes or root stocks each February and give a similar quantity at planting time.

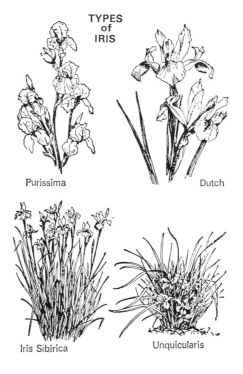

TYPES of IRIS

Purissima

Dutch

Iris Sibirica

Unquicularis

The Beardless or Apogon group have to be divided into large numbers of sections, i.e. the bulbous irises, the Stylosa group, the Spuria or moisture-loving group, the Kaempferi or Japanese group, the Evansia or Crested group and so on. Those who are going in for cultivating these types would do well to study a book which deals with irises only.

Bearded Irises. The normal iris garden is planted up with the bearded types. These vary in height, form and colour but flower very much at the same period. There are it is true the dwarf bearded irises that flower in March and April and the Intermediates that flower in April and early May, but the bulk of them flower at the end of May and beginning of June.

The colours have to be seen to be believed. There are blues and pinks, blends with yellow predominating; bronzes and browns, crimsons, pinks and lilac pinks, whites and creams pencilled with a darker colour; very often the main petals are one colour and the falls another. The following are some of my favourites : Blue Rhythm, a cornflower blue; Tint o' Tan, a buff and tan; New Snow, a pure white; Olakala, a deep golden yellow; Golden Fleece, a lemon and white; Great Lakes, a light blue; Paradise Pink, a flamingo pink; Garden Magic, a red with orange beard; Deep Black, a dark purple; Shah Jehan, a pale yellow and bronze edged; Staton Island, a gold and maroon; Watermeads, a grey white and deep blue; Chantelly, an orchid pink; Pace Maker, a dusky red; Marco Polo, a rose and crimson; Sable, a violet purple; Lady Mohr, a primrose and lavender; Proem, a blue shot old gold; Sweet Alibi, a creamy yellow; Especially You, the darkest yellow I know; Sandia, a shell pink; Stained Glass, a bronzy red.

Of course there are lots of others I could have mentioned but those I have given you are delightful to grow.

Dwarf Bearded Irises. In this group I can recommend a few : Orange Queen, 6 in. high; Princess Louise, 6 in.; Cœrulea, 6 in.; Moonlight, 4 in.; Blue Pygmy, 6 in.; Amber Queen, 9 in.

Intermediate Bearded Irises. Here are one or two to include in your list : Aquamarine, a blue; Golden West, a yellow; Moonbeam, a yellow; Cæsar's Brother, a deep purple, 3 ft; Perry's Blue, 3 ft; Emperor, a violet blue; Tropic Night, dark purple.

Propagation. Bearded irises are easy to divide. The outer rhizomes may be severed with one or two strong roots attached and these can be replanted in another position. It is always advisable in the case of large clumps to discard the inferior and older portions. The division should be done immediately after the plants have flowered. This means that they will be transplanted late in June and early

in July, usually the driest period of the year. For this reason some gardeners wait until early September but if you
do this the roots will have started to grow well and will
only be injured.

Planting the Border. Plant the border naturally so that you
have five or six bearded irises of one particular variety in
a group. Stick to the main principles advised in the planting of the herbaceous border (see page 37). Drift the
lighter blues into the darker ones and so on into the tall
growing mauves at the back of the border. Keep the
dwarfer irises to the front as as a rule, but every now and
then bring a taller one to the front to break up the monotony. Remember if you do go in for a iris border you must
be prepared for it to be dull at certain seasons of the year.
It can, however, be very beautiful indeed.

Night-scented Border

In the daytime the garden is there to be seen and admired
but in the evening when the shadows fall the bright flowers
have lost their power and it is then that a garden can be
'felt'. The scents that arise can bring about a sense of
enchantment and a walk in the garden at night-time can
be, as a result, more entrancing than a stroll during the
glories of midday. Plant with a view to making one border
at least, or part of a border, a scented one, and see how
the luminous petals of the Evening Primroses glow palely
and the scented drift of the Mrs. Sinkins pinks pervade
the air.

In the case of crazy paving it is always useful to plant
up the interspaces with the scented thyme which has a
carpeting-like effect and gives off a lovely scent when trodden on. There are a number of these baby thymes. Ask your
nurseryman about them. Along the front of the border you
can have the Night-scented Stock. Do not have too much
of it in one spot or it looks untidy in the daytime. Mix it
with Virginia Stock and you have brightness in the day
and fragrance at night. I like to have the Night-scented
Stock in a narrow bed close to the study window and its
perfume is wafted into the room.

Another plant that does well is the *Œnothera odorata*.
This grows about 4 ft high and bears buff flowers. It gives
off plenty of perfume. Close by, plant a drift of the Dame's
Violet or Sweet Rocket as it is often called. It can easily
be grown from seed and will produce spikes 2 ft long, the

top 10 in. of which will be covered with white or purplish flowers according to variety.

There is a dwarfer type known as Delicate Mauve, which grows nearly 18 in. tall but is just as highly scented. The Tobacco plants give much perfume in the evening hours. *Nicotiana affinis* looks rather unbecoming during the day because its flowers are closed. *Nicotiana suaveolens* only grows 18 in. high, the pure white flowers being over 1½ in. across. This is the variety usually used for the greenhouse.

Other plants that may be grown for their scent are the Monarda or Bergamot with its scarlet flowers and scented leaves; Balm with its delightfully lemon scented foliage; Lavender; the Lemon-scented Verbena; Sweet Briar Roses; the Veronica cupressoides, which smell of cedar wood, and Rosemary which has a subtle smell of the bay.

The Aster Border (Michaelmas Daisies)

The Michaelmas Daisies do well in a border on their own, and the bulk of them are in flower in October, when the rest of the garden is rather bare. It is quite excusable to have a special border for these flowers when the garden is big enough. In the normal way, however, the Michaelmas Daisies will be planted in the herbaceous border and so will extend the flowering season.

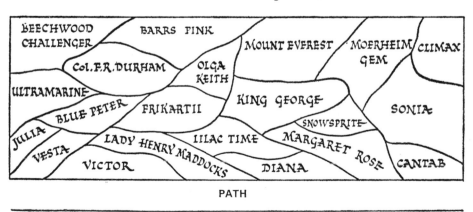

PATH

A good Michaelmas Daisy border might be planned so that it would be in bloom, say, from the middle of September to the second wek of November, especially if it were possible to have this aster garden in a sheltered spot, where the plants would not be battered by the late autumn winds.

Any ordinary soil will suit the perennial aster. It should be well dug and manured for the roots of this family go down deply on the whole. A liberal dressing of composted vegetable refuse, say at one bucketful per sq. yard, may be dug in a spade's depth, plus a dressing of organic fertilizer as advised for irises. Michaelmas Daisy borders will not be down for more than two or three years and most of the taller free-flowering varieties insist on being split up every two years. Perennial asters may be increased by root division carried out in the autumn directly after flowering. With the taller varieties strong pea sticks should be used, pushed into the ground around and among the plants, so that the growth can develop naturally and yet be supported.

VARIETIES. Of course it is impossible to give a complete list of all the varieties there are and so I mention a few of the best.

ASTER ACRIS. 2-3 ft, lilac blue flowers, August-Sep-

ASTER ACRIS. 2-3 ft, lilac blue flowers, August-September.

ASTER AMELLUS. This group varies from 2-3½ ft. King George, flowers 3 in. across, blue. Sonia, bright pink, large flowers. Frikartii, large light blue flowers, late August-early October.

ASTER ERICOIDES. 2½ ft, tiny flowers, heath-like foliage. Brimstone with lovely baby yellow flowers. Cinderella, 3 ft, erect and branching, blue. Ring Dove, 2½ ft, October, lavender.

ASTER NOVÆ-ANGLIÆ. 4-5 ft, large flowers, generally coloured. Harrigton's Pink, a very free grower. September Ruby, deep rosy red flowers, excellent cut flower.

ASTER NOVÆ-BELGII. The tallest section of all. Many plants are over 6 ft. Ada Ballard, mauvy-blue, early September, 4½ ft. Beechwood Challenger, the finest red I know, September, 3½ ft. Moderator, semi-double rich mauve, September. Freda Ballard, exquisite double red flowers, October. Royal Ruby, a glowing ruby red, 3½ ft, October. Royal Velvet, a deep violet blue with golden centre, September. Lady Frances, a semi-double deep pink, October. Climax, a light blue with gold centre, 5 ft.

ASTER DWARF HYBRIDS. (Largely introduced by

my friend, the late Major H. Victor Vokes.) Victor, a clear pale lavender blue, 6 in. Margaret Rose, a semi-double bright rose-pink. Blue Bouquet, a bright blue. Dandy, a purple red. Gayborder Charm, semi-double mauve. Jenny, a double violet-purple, 12 in. Lilac Time, blue, 9 in. Red Boy, rosy red. Pink Lace, double pink, 15 in. Rose Bonnet, misty pink. Snowsprite, white, 12 in.

The Dahlia Border

Dahlias have become very popular during the last few years and many people like to have special borders devoted to their culture. Many parks devote quite large areas to dahlias today, and I have found these beds just as popular in the north as in the south. Dahlias can be divided up into groups, for instance the Singles, the Anemone-flowered, the Collarette, the Pæony-flowered, the Giant Decorative, the Miniature Decorative, the Pom-pom, the Cactus, the Semi-Cactus and the Miniature Balls. Most dahlia catalogues show quite clearly to which group particular varieties belong. Sometimes they show this by the letters 'C' meaning Cactus, 'SC' semi-Cactus, 'D' Decorative and so on.

Dahlias like to be planted in an open position where they can get full sun. The ground in which they are to be planted should be dug over, and dung or well-rotted vegetable refuse should not be added at the same time. This should be given as a top dressing early in June. The planting cannot be done till all danger of frost is over but it is quite convenient to mark the position of each plant with a small tick beforehand. The strong decorative or cactus sorts will need to be 4 ft apart. The pæony-flowered, small decoratives and collarettes 3 ft apart, with the dwarfer varieties of these types 2 ft apart.

The bedding dahlias will only need about 1 ft of room. The gardener's aim should be to have such a mass of bloom that it hides the soil below. Dahlias should always be planted firmly and if the weather is warm and dry each plant should be watered in. Do not give the plants any nitrogenous fertilizer. Work into the top 2 or 3 in. of soil bone meal at 3-4 oz to the sq. yard and wood ash at half a pound to the sq. yard.

Stake the varieties early with strong bamboos, but in such a way that the foliage hides the supports. The dwarfer varieties may be supported by the use of dwarf pea sticks put in among them as they are growing. When the plants are in full flower, it is quite a good plan to feed with a liquid manure say once a fortnight.

Dahlias will continue flowering till they are cut down by frost in the autumn. The old stems should then be cut to within 6 in. of soil level and the roots lifted carefully with a fork. The tubers should be dried thoroughly before storing. They may be placed in boxes having been well labelled first and are then usually covered with sand or dry peat. The usual plan is to place them stem downwards to prevent the moisture settling round the tops of the tubers at the base of the stem where the dormant eyes, which will produce next year's shoots, are to be found. Dahlia roots should be stored during the winter in some building which is dry and frostproof.

Varieties

There must surely be thousands of varieties of dahlias and I can do no more than mention a few of my favourites. Every year new varieties are introduced and those who are keen on dahlias should obtain catalogues from the specialist dahlia nurseries. To remind you, the abbreviations are as follows :

(Col.) Colerette, (S.S.C.) Semi-cactus small, (P.F.) Paeony Flowered, (G.D.) Giant Decorative, (S.D.) Small Decorative, (S.C.) Semi-cactus, (C.) Cactus, (M.S.C.) Medium Semi-cactus, (M.C.) Miniature Cactus, (P.) Pom pom, (B.D.) Bedding Dahlia.

			Ht. Ft.
Amethyst	(S.D.)	Nearest to blue dahlia ...	4½
Andreas Moderna	(M.S.C.)	Salmon-yellow ...	3-3½
Baby Royal	(M.C.)	Pale rose-pink with apricot shadings	4½
Beauty of Achsmeer	(M.S.C.)	Deep Salmon, darker centre	4½
Bishop of Llandaff	(P.F.)	Rich Scarlet, with dark foliage	2
Border Princess	(S.C. Dw.B)	Salmon bronze	
Chimboraso	(Col.)	Maroon and yellow ...	
Colonel W. M. Ogg	(G.D.)	Cream sport from Major Messervy ...	3½-4
Corydon	(S.D.)	Clear Salmon, strong stem	3½
Chirrup	S.S.C.)	Magenta rose tipped cream	3½
David Howard	(Min. D.)	Deep bronze, leaves almost black	3½
Doris Day	(S.C.)	Cardinal red	3½
Daily Mail	(G.D.)	Large yellow and orange	4-4½
Curtain Raiser	(M.C.)	Salmon orange ...	4
Ehrenpreis	(M.S.C.)	Fine salmon-rose ...	3½-4
Evelyn Rumbold	(G.D.)	Fine lilac-purple	4
Hamari Saffron	(M.S.C.)	Saffron-yellow	4½

			Ht. Ft.
Florissant	(Col.)	Pink with white edge ...	4
G. K. Moltke	(S.D.)	Lovely shade of salmon	3-3½
Gina Lombeart	(M.S.C.)	Salmon and yellow ...	4
Hamari Boldness	(L.D.)	Deep velvet red	4½
Good Intent	(Min. Ba.)	Clear lavender	3
Jhr. van Citters	(P.)	Old gold tipped bronze-red	3
Jocondo	(G.D.)	Bright reddish-purple ...	4
Knightsbridge	(M.D.)	Golden yellow	4½
Lemon Beauty	(Charm)	Lemon-yellow ...	3½-4
Little Conn	(P.)	Crimson-scarlet	3½
Little Wills	(M.C.)	Fine orange - amber with yellow centre ...	3-3½
Maureen Creighton	(B.D.)	Fine double scarlet ...	1½-2
Mrs. J. C. Sowton	(G.D.)	Large pinkish cinnamon	3½
Neil Lewis	(S.D.)	Orange-yellow	4
Muriel Gladwell	(S.S.C.)	Tomato juice colour ...	4
Polly Peachum	(S.D.)	Purple overlaid rose ...	4½
Prairie Fire	(S.D.)	Signal red	4
Pwll Coch	(S.S.C.)	Scarlet red	3½
Pink Mark	(G.D.)	Fine cyclamen-pink ...	3
Quel Diable	(M.S.C.)	Deep orange	4
Raisers Pride	(M.C).	Salmon-pink	4½
Rotterdam	(H.S.C.)	Crimson-red	4
Sally Jane	(S.D.	Pink and creamy-yellow ...	4
Scottish Import	(S.L.)	Crimson-red	3½
Swiss Miss	(Min. Ba.)	Pink tipped white ...	3½
Trelawny	(G.D.)	Lovely bronze-red, huge ..	4½
Trendy	(S.D.)	Yellow and cerise ...	3
White Swallow	(S.S.C.)	Pure white	3½
Winifred	(S.D.)	Very bright red ...	3-3½
Yes Sir	(M.D.)	Lilac pink	4½

Chrysanthemums

Many people make a speciality of chrysanthemums. Chrysanthemums can be grown in the normal herbaceous border, but very often they are given a plot of ground on their own, especially by those who specialize in this group for cut flowers for the house.

The best soil for chrysanthemums would seem to be a good loam of good depth. It should be prepared by shallow digging in the autumn and properly composed vegetable refuse should be incorporated at 2 large bucketfuls to the sq. yard. Into the top 2 in. should be forked medium grade sedge peat at 1 bucketful to the sq. yard, this being damped beforehand should the soil be dry and sandy. Fish manure should be used a 3 oz to the sq. yard, with the peat, plus wood ashes at 6 oz to the sq. yard.

Before planting see that the ground is firm, either by treading or a light rolling. In the case of heavy soil it may be firm enough without any particular treatment. Plant with a trowel so that you can make a good hole to take the ball of roots. Plant firmly and give a good watering at planting time if the soil is dry. In the south it is usually possible to plant about the third week of April but in the north it is often advisable to delay until the middle of May unless the plants can be covered by continuous cloches. If the border is being planted for beauty then drifts of various varieties can be arranged as advised for Michaelmas Daisies but if it is merely a question of cut flowers then it is usual to have the plants 1 ft apart in the rows and 18 in. apart between the rows. It is convenient to have 4 rows 18 in. apart, and the 2 ft wide break for a path, another 4 rows and so on.

To get early flowering it is often necessary to pinch out the growing points of the plants in order to cause them to break early. For instance, I have had plants that have been 'stopped' as it is called, on May 20th, and which flowered in consequence on August 20th. The same variety in the same bed when not stopped broke naturally on June 15th and did not flower till September 15th in consequence. Chrysanthemums need supports and bamboos are usually

The right way to disbud chrysanthemums.

used for this purpose, 4-5 ft bamboo being put into the ground at planting time. Keep the ground hoed regularly unless the area where the Chrysanthemums are being grown is mulched completely with sedge peat an inch deep, when hoeing is unnecessary as the annual weeds cannot grow. Tie the plants up to the bamboos as they grow. Where large flowers are required disbudding should be done. This consists of removing the small flower buds on the side of the stems and so concentrating the energies of the plant on the main flower bud at the end of each stem.

Varieties. Again I only mention a few favourites of mine. Keep an eye on the catalogues and make notes of recent introductions. Try and see them at shows.

Rockall, a pink and silver incurved.

Martin Riley, a yellow incurved.

Primrose Cricket, a beautiful primrose.

Lady Anna, a rosy lilac.

Ruby Queen, a rich crimson.

Shirley Victoria, a chestnut amber.

Garden Choice, a salmon pink.

Gladys Homer, a golden amber reflexed.

Violets

Some like to grow violets as cut flowers, but not every soil is suitable for violet growing. Light soils have a tendency to get too dry and make the plants liable to red spider. Heavy soils may be too wet. It is a medium type of soil that is required. See that the land concerned is well drained, if heavy, and properly enriched with plenty of compost if light. Violets dislike acid soils and so lime must be applied. Choose a situation where there is good protection on the east and north side to keep out cold winds.

Having forked in sedge peat lightly or even well-rotted compost, get the soil down to a very fine tilth in the spring and plant with a trowel. In the south much planting is done in April but in the north it will often be delayed until mid-May. It is usual to allow 14 in. from plant to plant, though double varieties may be planted in the 1 ft square principle.

Keep the violet beds clean and free from weeds all the year round by mulching the ground where they are growing with compost or sedge peat and be prepared to water with the hose with a good deal of pressure behind, so as to flood and keep the foliage damp. The earliest of the plants should begin to flower towards the end of September and from early November onwards it is worth while covering the violets with cloches or frames. In the north it is usually necessary to lift the plants with a ball of soil to their roots and plant them in a frame 2 ft square. The frame should face south. It should be filled with soil to 10 in. of the top, which should run parallel to the frame light. After planting, soak the ground well but do not cover over with the frame lights until the frost appears.

Propagation. In the spring, runners will have grown on the flowering plants. These root in a similar manner to strawberries. When rooted, sever them from their parent plants and put out in their permanent position.

Sometimes runners are removed in September, and these are planted out in cold frames or under cloches 2 in. apart. They are given shade until they have established themselves. Such plants are ready to put out in their permanent position in March in the south and in May in the north.

Varieties.

Admiral Avalon, a reddish-purple.

Governor Herrick, a deep purple; large flower, no scent. Red spider resister, however.

Marie Louise, a double mauve, good scent.

Comte de Brazza, the best double white.

Sweet Peas

Sweet Peas are often grown in clumps up tall twiggy pea sticks in the flower border. On other occasions they are grown on the cordon system up single bamboos and are dis-shooted carefully. They may easily grow to 8 ft in height and should be in flower during June and July. The most convenient way of sowing the seed is to do it under cloches out of doors during October. This saves any transplanting. Some like to raise plants in pots in the greenhouse and then transplant the seedlings thus raised late in April. Others just sow the seed in the spring in the borders where the plants are to grow; for early flowering and long stems it is necessary to sow in the autumn, either indoors or out.

The ground where the Sweet Peas are to grow should be shallowly dug and properly composted vegetable refuse should be applied at the rate of one bucketful to the sq. yard. When the ground is being prepared for seed sowing or planting a good fish manure should be added at 3 oz to the sq. yard plus finely divided wood ashes at 8 oz to the sq. yard. A skittering of hydrated lime will be given to the surface of the soil.

Once the plants are growing well, compost or sedge peat will be placed along the rows to a depth of 2 or 3 in. and

to a width of 6 in. or so on either side, to act as a mulch.
Once the flowers have formed, feeding with Marinure may
be done once a fortnight in accordance with the instructions given on the bottle. After planting it is usual to stop
the Sweet Peas by cutting off the growing point at just
above the second leaf. When the seeds are sown "in situ"
this is generally done when the plants are 3 in. high. Side
growths thus break out from the base of the plants and two
of these will be retained. These are generally stronger than
the main growth.

The great thing is to give the plants firm support. They
hate growing up unsteady stakes or swaying boughs, or
string. When growing on the cordon system, pinch back
all the side shoots as they appear and cut off the tendrils.
Some people keep the main growth tied to the bamboos
by the use of wire split rings. Others make loose ties.

Varieties. The following varieties are typical of the best kinds
to grow :

Snocap.   A large pure white.
Red Admiral.   Dark blood red.
Sun Dance.   Orange salmon.
Air Warden.   Orange cerise.
Lavender Lace.   Lavender.
Bouquet.   Mauve.
Carnival.   Cyclamen rose.
Hunters Moon.   Deep cream.
Modesty.   A light china pink.
Delice.   A soft pink overlaid salmon.
Carlotta.   A rosy carmine.
Signal.   A bright crimson with a sheen.
Leamington.   A sweetly scented lilac.
Duchess of Bedford.   A frilly light lavender blue.
Air Warden.   An almost orange scarlet.
Red Admiral.   A large flowered dark blood red.
Princess Elizabeth.   A salmon pink on creamy buff.
Spotlight.   An old ivory, flushed pink.
Mrs. R. Bolton.   A rich rose pink.
Noel Sutton.   A frilled deep-mid-blue.
Pixie.   A deep cream-marbled orange salmon.

15 Making and Stocking the Pool

Making a Garden Pool. Garden pools often become just a muddy pond because it is not realized that Nature insists on the 'correct balance'. A pool can either be formal or informal. It is often quite suitably placed at the bottom of the lawn or near the house as an adjunct to a paved pathway or court. Sometimes it is close to the rock garden and often connected to it by a small stream. Those who only have a small garden may like to make a pool by just sinking a tub into the ground. Never use a barrel that has contained soap, oil or petrol.

The informal pool will be of any shape desired and is generally made to fit into the plan or picture of the garden. If it is intended to stock the pond with fish, shade is necessary, but this should be provided either by tall, marginal plants or by floating aquatics. The dish-shaped pool is easiest to make. The soil should be dug out to the right depth and the soft places filled in with clinker or rubble to get a firm even base. The concrete which should consist of 1 part cement and 3 parts sand should then be 'spread' over the depression provided to a depth of at least 3 in. Cover the soil with newspaper first before placing the concrete in position, as this prevents to soil from absorbing the water from the concrete. A pond can thus be made to any shape but its size should not exceed 4 ft in diameter and the depth not greater than 18 in. Otherwise difficulties always arise when placing the concrete in position.

A good pool is one which is rectangular and provides water at varying depths, one end being, say, 12 in. deeper than the other. It is also desirable to provide a ledge about 12 in. wide and 4 in. below the normal water level so that the baby fish find a hiding place during the spawning season. The thickness of the concrete will probably be 4 in. in this case. When the position of the pool and the design have been decided on, the soil excavation has to be carried out. Again the bottom of the pool must be rammed and levelled to provide a firm even base. The bottom of the pool should be concreted if possible in one operation and it is advisable to drive timber pegs at intervals across the width and length of the pond, the tops of which should be level with the desired thickness of concrete. The concrete should be composed of 1 part cement, 2 parts sand and 3 parts shingle, graded from $\frac{3}{4}$ in. down to 3/16 in.

MAKING A GARDEN POOL

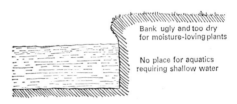

Bank ugly and too dry
for moisture-loving plants

No place for aquatics
requiring shallow water

Earth removed
and deposited in water creating moist
banks and shallow margins

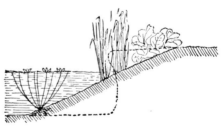

Right and Wrong
kinds of margins for ponds and streams

The pegs should be removed as the work progresses and the top surface finished off with a wooden float. The edges of the bottom slab on which the side walls of the pool would rest should be roughened in order to form a 'key' between the sides and the bottom. Concreting should not be done in frosty weather. The sides of the pool should then be built up inside a timber framework which looks rather like a long, narrow, rectangular box, which has to be securely battened and braced to prevent the timber from bulging during the placing of the concrete.

The concrete is filled into the shuttering in even layers, working gradually round the pool and is consolidated with a stout piece of timber. The forms are then left in position for three days and during that period the concrete is kept wet. After this time the timbers are removed and the pond filled with water. Mark one side of the pool with a pencil at water level so that you cn see if any noticeable leaking takes place. Before the plants or the fish are introduced the inside of the pool must be seasoned and this means that the water must be left in for a couple of weeks and then the bottom and sides should be scrubbed vigorously with a hard brush. This process should be repeated two or three times.

Another method of seasoning consists of painting the inside of the pool with a 1 in 4 solution of waterglass three times at intervals of three days. Sometimes there are available green and blue bituminous paints which have the same effect, and make the pool look quite attractive when filled with water.

Soon after the pool has been stocked, the clarity of the water will disappear, but if the correct plants and livestock have been introduced to give the necessary balance, the water should clear in a few months and keep clear ever afterwards. Consult a good aquatic nurseryman before starting the pool. You will need floating aquatics, oxygenating plants, ordinary aquatics, ferns or rushes, plus fish, crustacea and insects. The waste matter which accumulates in a pool is considerable and it is essential that the right plants and 'animals' are there to absorb this material. One plant is usually necessary to every square foot and it is generally necessary to layer the pond with a good loam spread in the bottom to a depth of 6 in. This should be well rammed.

Water Lilies. Water Lilies should be planted after the middle of April and during May and June. Firm planting is essential. Pressure should be applied around the roots. To prevent the plants from rising as the water runs into the pool place large stones around the plants and leave them in position for, say, six weeks. It is always better to cover the plants with only a few inches of water until growth commences and then as the plants progress the pool may be filled. If hardy species of water lilies are grown, they will stand all the frosts experienced in this country. There are many different varieties of water lilies. Some need 12 in. of water and will cover an area of 24 in., others need 2 or 3 ft of water and will cover an area of from 7 to 10 ft.

Good varieties for small pools are :

CHRYSANTHA. A yellow tinged with red.

GRAZIELLA. A coppery-red to orange yellow.

TETRAGONA ALBA. A white which can be grown in a pool only 6 in. deep and 15 in. across.

For the larger pools I recommend :

ATROPURPUREA. A deep crimson with yellow stamens.

INDIANA. A yellowy-orange to coppery-red.

JAMES BRYDON. A crimson pink with golden stamens.

COLOSSEA. Very large pale pink flowers from May until October. It needs plenty of room.

Aquatic Plants. There are a large number of aquatic plants that can be planted around the margin of the water garden or in more central positions in the pool. Some prefer to be covered with about 5 in. of water with their foliage under and their flowers on or above; others like the same depth of water and have their foliage and flowers above water. Some float and require no soil at all. These usually have to be wintered in a greenhouse. Some like to be covered with 12-15 in. of water and have both foliage and flowers floating on the surface. Study a good aquatic catalogue and make your choice.

I can recommend the following for your consideration :

THE WATER GLADIOLI.

THE WATER FORGET-ME-NOT.

THE MANNA GRASS.

THE REED MACE.

THE WATER HAWTHORN.

THE WATER POPPY.

THE MARSH MARIGOLD.

THE WATER IRIS.

THE WATER MUSK.

Submerged Oxygenators. The submerged oxygenating plants are most essential. They absorb the carbon dioxide and retain the carbon for their own growth, returning the oxygen to the water for use by other plants. They work every day to keep the water clear. Submerged aquatics provide the necessary shade and shelter for young fish. Some of them are a source of food for the fish and provide them with the mineral salts they require. Be careful never to introduce duckweed or azolla into a pool.

Good submerged oxygenating aquatics are :
WATER MILFOIL.
WATER STARWORT.
WATER VIOLET.
WATER LOBELIA. Likes shallow water.
WATER CROWSFOOT.

The Fish

Fish help to ensure the correct balance of Nature and are most attractive when swimming about in the water. Don't, however, have too many fish. You need 1 in. of fish to each gallon of water. It is always better to understock a pool to allow for increase in weight. Fish should have the opportunity of swimming a length which is eight times their own length. Fish, when put into the water, should all be approximately the same size. Always purchase fish for a pool which have already been living in a pool. Never buy fish from a large lake or running stream. Fish eat less in winter than in the summer. It is only necessary in the winter months to give a pinch of fish food on a sunny day. In the summer they should be fed regularly and a good time is early in the evening. It is a good plan to stock the pool with water fleas and lice for these being rich in protein provide the fishes with food. Small red worms may be given and fresh ant eggs, but not the dried eggs which are sold for the purpose.

Goldfish should be bought direct from an English breeder and there are various varieties available. Discuss these with the supplier.

Scavengers. Stock the pool with sufficient scavengers to devour the decaying vegetation. You should have no more than one water snail per 5 gallons of water. Introduce fresh water lice but never fish lice. Water fleas are useful but again these should be purchased and not collected from a pond in the country.

Never introduce leeches. The fresh water whelk breeds prolifically and scavenges well. My favourite, however, is the Ramshorn snail.

The specialist aquatic nurseryman will always advise the beginner as to the number of each type of plant to use, plus the right number of fish, scavengers and 'fleas'.

I have found that a tub 30 in. across and 18 in. deep will accommodate 4 goldfish, 4 oxygenating plants, plus, say, three aquatic plants of the type that throw both flowers and foliage well above water level, plus a sprinkling of scavengers and 'food' insects.

16 What to do Month by Month

January

Bastard trench land intended for new flower borders.

Lightly fork over surface of existing herbaceous borders.

Plant shrubs of all kinds.

Plant herbaceous perennials.

Tread perennials in that were planted in November or December, after a thaw.

Get catalogue from the seedsman and order your annuals.

Protect hairy foliaged alpines with sheets of glass over them, held in position, 6 in. above, by clips.

Prepare land for sweet peas.

Prepare land for dahlias and chrysanthemums.

Rake dead leaves and rubbish off rock gardens and shrubberies.

February

Build a new rock garden.

Make a garden pool.

Plant hardy perennials.

Plant roses.

Thin growths of climbing roses.

Firm plants of winter bedding, loose in soil.

Lift and divide perennials if necessary.

Protect early flowering irises.

March

Sow seeds of many hardy annuals in the south.

Sow sweet peas.

Complete the planting of hardy perennials.

Thin out autumn sown annuals.

Complete the planting of roses or hardy shrubs.

Start pruning rose trees towards the end of the month.

Plant out carnations that have been over-wintering in frames.

Start giving support to perennials towards the end of the month.

Give top dressing of compost if necessary in rock garden.

Top dress azaleas and rhododendrons with sedge peat.

Plant corms of gladioli.

Plant hardy types of lilies.

Protect young perennials from slugs by using Draza pellets.

April

Sow seeds of hardy annuals (in north).

Continue sowing hardy annuals in south.

Sow 'baby' hardy annuals in pockets in rock garden.

Hoe perennial flower border.

Hoe shrubberies.

Plant out sweet peas raised in greenhouse.

In south plant out penstemons and calceolarias towards end of month.

Plant out violas which have been over-wintering in frames.

Plant out pansies.

Thin out hardy annuals sown earlier.

Complete the pruning of roses.

Plant out alpines in rock garden.

Plant early flowering chrysanthemums towards the end of the month in south.

Prune back rampant growing rock plants.

Feed polyanthuses and auriculas with Marinure.

Plant out the hollyhocks.

Take basal growths of perennials and strike as cuttings in sandy soil covered with cloches.

Pinch dead flowers off pansies and violas regularly.

Sow seeds of sweet scented annuals.

May

Plant out early flowering chrysanthemums in north.

Plant out dahlias after the middle of the month.

Sow hardy annuals for successional flowering.

Sow seeds of polyanthus and auriculas for flowering next spring.

Lift and divide polyanthus after flowering.

Hoe through flower borders regularly.

Pull up the winter bedding plants after the middle of the month. They should have by then finished flowering.

Get the borders prepared for summer bedding plants.

After the 15th of the month plant out half-hardy annuals.

See that the bedding plants are well watered towards the end of the month if the weather is dry.

Seeds of half-hardy annuals may be sown out of doors about the second week.

Sow seeds of the biennials about the middle of the month, i.e. forget-me-nots, canterbury bells, wallflowers, etc.

Tie in the rambler rose shoots as they start to grow, to prevent them being damaged.

Keep cutting off dead flower heads in the rock garden.

Remove all the seeding heads from rhododendrons and other similar shrubs.

Cut down the early flowering plants in the herbaceous border.

Continue lifting polyanthus and auriculas. Divide them and transplant to a nursery bed.

Thin out all the annuals sown earlier to give them plenty of room to grow.

June

Cut roses and sweet peas regularly to keep them flowering.

Cut the anchusas, delphiniums and lupins to the ground – immediately they have finished flowering.

Sow seeds of biennials like wallflowers, forget-me-nots and alyssum about the middle of the month for winter bedding – if not already done.

Propagate arabis, aubretia and alyssum by cuttings put in sandy soil in a shady border.

If the weather is dry, water the annuals thoroughly.

If droughty, water the newly-planted bedding stuff *thoroughly*.

See that the rock garden is thoroughly watered in dry weather.

Keep the rose beds soaked if dry and you will help to prevent mildew.

Prune earlier flowering hardy shrubs about the end of the month.

Sow seeds of some of the perennials.

Cut the flowers regularly in the cut flower border and the plants will go on flowering.

Thin out and transplant annuals sown in the spring.

Transplant biennials 6 in. square from earlier sowings.

Protect catmint (*Nepeta mussini*) from cats.

Cut back rampaging growing plants in rock garden.

Propagate certain perennials like anchusas, phlox and delphiniums by means of root cuttings.

Pinch out the main growths of clarkias, godetias and helichrysums to make them branch out.

Propagate pinks by cuttings or pipings inserted in sandy soil.

Propagate pansies and iberis by cuttings.

Keep spraying with a good nicotine wash to keep down pests.

Keep using Draza pellets and fine bone meal to control slugs if necessary.

Keep training climbing roses as the new growths develop.

July

Continue propagating alyssum and arabis by cuttings.

Many rock plants may be propagated by cuttings in sandy soil in a frame.

Continue propagating pinks by pipings.

Feed the roses once every three weeks with Marinure if necessary.

Feed the sweet peas in a similar manner.

Sow more wallflowers if necessary.

Keep cutting flowers regularly in cut flower border.

Lift the sweet williams and canterbury bells when over. Plant the spaces with late bedding plants.

Cut the pansies back hard and replant if necessary in a reserve garden.

Remove seed heads from all flowers in herbaceous border.

Stake and tie up all dahlias and thin out growths if necessary.

Support border chrysanthemums, and disbud them for large blooms.

Continue to hoe through flower borders and shrub borders.

August

If going on holiday this month, cut down all flowering plants before you go.

Make notes of the herbaceous border with a view to re-planning in the winter.

Feed sweet peas and roses with Marinure.

Remove all suckers from around rose bushes.

Plant out Brompton stocks.

Plant bulbs in wild garden.

Plant out seedling pansies to make an edge for a border.

Keep hoeing all flower and shrub borders.

Prepare beds for planting narcissus, daffodils, tulips, etc.

Propagate pansies from cuttings.

Propagate violas from cuttings.

Take cuttings from fuchsias.

Thin out growths of Michaelmas daisies for better blooms.

Take rose cuttings.

Layer outdoor carnations.

September

Make a list of the climbers, perennials, or bulbs you will need and order them right away.

Keep cutting the flowers regularly in the cut flower border.

Keep thinning out the growths of Michaelmas daisies if necessary.

See that all late flowering plants like chrysanthemums, dahlias and Michaelmas daisies are properly staked and supported.

Plant the polyanthuses in their flowering positions.

About the middle of the month sow hardy annuals that will over-winter.

Sweep up all leaves and put on the compost heap to rot down.

Cut the suckers from roses right to their base.

Cut back rampant growths of climbers, wistaria, clematis or roses if necessary.

Take cuttings of pentstemons, calceolarias or alyssum in a frame or under cloches.

Sever carnation layers and replant.

Plant out pink pipings or cuttings which should now be 'struck'.

Keep spraying with a good derris wash to keep down pests.

Keep hoeing flower borders and flowering shrub borders.

October

When frost ruins them, cut down dahlias, lift the roots and store.

Take up summer bedding and replant with winter or spring bedding.

It is now time to plant forget-me-nots, polyanthuses, wallflowers, Canterbury bells, arabis, etc.

This is the month for planting bulbs.

This is a good month for planting alpines in the rock garden.

Cut down perennial plants in the herbaceous border directly they have finished flowering.

Keep sweeping up fallen leaves and put on the compost heap to rot down.

Plant new roses as soon as possible.

Remove all 'dead' matter from rock garden.

Lift tender plants and put into frame or cover with continuous cloches.

November

Protect Christmas roses with cloches.

Plant flowering trees and shrubs.

Plant many kinds of evergreen shrubs.

Plant roses and climbers of all kinds.

Make new herbaceous borders.

Make new shrub borders.

Continue to plant bulbs during the first week.

Protect the tender herbaceous plants in the border by covering with cloches or surrounding them with old ashes. It is often damp around the crown that causes the trouble.

December

Start grubbing up the shrubs you do not require.

Rake over the shrub border, remove leaves and put on compost heap.

Continue to plant the roses and climbers.

Dig up and replant an old herbaceous border if not already done.

Cover autumn sown annuals with cloches or put pea sticks among them to break the cold winds.

Remove heavy quantities of snow from bushes or climbers if likely to break the branches.

Look through the flower seed catalogues as soon as they arrive and send in your order.

Remake and replant any reserve flower border you may have.

See that sheets of glass are protecting the fluffy-leaved plants in the rock garden. The sheets should be held 6 in. above the plants with special clips that can be bought for the purpose.

A number of pests and diseases attack nearly all plants, so I will deal with these first. Then I will deal briefly with the troubles that attack individual flowering plants in the garden.

Pests and Diseases

Wireworms. This is the larva of the click beetle. It is browny yellow in colour, very wiry and may be distinguished from millipedes and centipedes by the fact that it has only 3 pairs of legs situated in the first 3 segments of its body. Millipedes and centipedes have legs all down their bodies. Wireworms will stay in the ground for 5 or 6 years; so if you have trouble in your flower garden it is worth while spending money to get rid of it.

CONTROL. The simplest way of doing this is to make holes with a walking stick or crowbar, 2 ft apart all over the area of ground concerned, and drops into the bottom of these holes a piece of of paradichlorobenzene the size of a French bean. Tread down the holes immediately afterwards.

Earwigs. Some people consider these very serious pests but others say they do little harm. If earwigs are found in large numbers in any garden they should be destroyed. They are often a serious pest from the month of August onwards.

CONTROL. With 5 per cent Derris or Pyrethrum -- or both -- dust all round the outsides of gardens and along the edges of paths where the earwigs collect.

Inverting flower-pots stuffed with straw, hay or wood wool on bamboos stood among plants is the old-fashioned method of trapping them. In the morning the straw is removed and the earwigs collected there are shaken out into a bucket of paraffin.

Slugs and Snails. There are, unfortunately, many different kinds, some of which are more numerous than others. The slugs may be classified as follows :

1. The Large Black Slug, which is less commonly injurious to plants, but sometimes causes damage.

2. The Garden Slug, a small dark species with a yellow foot and a very tough skin, common both in gardens and fields.

3. The White-soled Slug, also a small species, generally grey in colour with a flattened appearance and with a strikingly white foot.

4. The Field Slug, variable in colour but usually mottled grey with a reddish or yellow tinge -- probably the most uniformly and generally injurious slug throughout the country.

5. The Keeled Slug – dark brown or grey with body keeled along the back. Very troublesome species, largely subterranean in habit, feeding on the underground parts of plants and often specially injurious to potatoes.

The two principal snails are :

1. The Large Garden Snail, the most common and widely distributed species of snail, easily distinguishable by large brown-grey shell with paler markings.

2. The Banded Snail, more injurious to farm crops than to garden crops as a whole. The shell may be white, grey, pale yellow, pink or brown with one to five spiral darker bands.

Generally speaking, slugs and snails eat anything fresh and green and succulent. Some seem to prefer roots and tubers and so attack below ground – others go for the parts of the plant above ground level. The majority of the dirty work is done at night time, and during the day the pests hide in any damp dark spot. Slugs will burrow deep down during the winter in order to escape the frost. Snails, on the other hand, collect in large numbers in a dry sheltered place.

Slugs usually prefer soils rich in moisture – the heavy soils, clays, etc. They love a wet winter and go on feeding and doing damage all the time. Given a chance they will get into a frame or a greenhouse, for there they can play havoc all the winter. Unfortunately, they revel in organic matter, and when heavy dressings are given on land which is not sufficiently well limed, trouble occurs because the partially rotted vegetable refuse may provide food for them. All vegetable refuse should therefore be properly composted before being used as a mulch on the soil.

The gardener feels that slugs and snails have far too few natural enemies, but this not so. Birds eat them greedily, especially rooks, starlings and blackbirds. Ducks love them, and some people allow their Khaki Campbells or Indian Runners to roam the vegetable garden in the winter when there are few crops about to harm. Toads and moles eat slugs, whilst snails are devoured by thrushes.

Control Measures

Everyone knows about the arduous method of hand collection : placing used orange skin and grapefruit skins upside down on the soil – picking up the slugs that have collected under them – and putting them in a tin of paraffin. But there are much better schemes than that.

1 – Copper Sulphate and Lime Method. Use powdered copper sulphate and hydrated lime, mixed together in equal parts. Dig this mixture in when bastard trenching. It is quite safe to use 1 oz per sq. yard, and even slightly heavier dressings than this have been used. A second similar dressing may be worked in 15 days before sowing seeds or setting out plants. The danger is the copper sulphate, which when overdone may poison the soil.

2 – The Methiocarb Method. The most recent development in slug control has been the introduction of slug pellets containing methiocarb. The advantage of these is that under damp conditions they are more effective than slug pellets on other chemicals and it is, of course, under warm moist conditions that slugs are most active.

Methiocarb is available in a mini-size form of pellet under the trade name 'Draza'. The small size of the pellet allows wide coverage economically and provides a large number of baiting points per unit area. Additionally, the small size of the pellet is far less likely to attract the attention of domestic animals which increases their safety factor. As a further point, from the safety angle, they are dyed blue, a colour which birds do not associate with food.

'Draza' pellets should be sprinkled about 5 in. apart in areas where slugs are causing trouble or known to be active.

3 – The Barrier Method. Some of the copper sulphate and hydrated lime mixture may be used from time to time along the edge of flower gardens to prevent the passage of slugs on to one's own particular portion of ground.

By this means it is possible to prevent the slugs travelling from one allotment or garden to another.

If the beds of flowers are covered with sedge peat an inch deep, the slugs cannot move about on the soil and so they never attack the plants. At the 8-acre gardens at Arkley Manor, near Barnet, slugs never cause trouble because all the beds are properly mulched.

Thrips. Tiny little black creatures which are slender and elongated. Being only one twentieth to one thirtieth of an inch in length, they are very inconspicuous. They damage the petals of flowers particularly, and cause them to be marked with white streaks. They may distort the blooms and mottle the leaves. Sometimes they suck the sap from the tips of seedlings. The simplest way of telling if a plant is being attacked by thrips is to hold a clean handkerchief close to the plant and tap it, and see if any little black specks drop on to the material. These, if thrips, will be found to wriggle, and if examined with a magnifying glass will be seen to be as already described.

CONTROL. Spray with nicotine, dissolving 1 oz in 10 gallons of water. Soak the plants thoroughly with this on a warm day for preference. Spray three times at weekly intervals, so as to make certain of catching insects that may have hatched out late from eggs.

Eel Worms. Minute little worms invariable invisible to the naked eye. They are eel-shaped, with a body slightly tapering towards the head. Eggs are usually laid somewhere in the plant tissues. In the case of phlox, sweet williams and chrysanthemums the eel worm swims up the film of moisture around the stems and enters the leaves by their breathing pores.

The eel worm also attacks bulbs. It enters through the tip and lives in the bulb, breeding for long periods. The bulbs thus attacked produce short foliage, and flowers on short stem, if they flower at all. In bad attacks the bulbs become soft.

CONTROL. To kill the eel worm in the bulbs it is necessary to give a special warm water bath treatment, a rather difficult thing for amateurs to do.

With chrysanthemums it is possible to give the stools and roots a warm water bath at exactly 110°F. for 20 minutes just before they are put out into the frames or boxes to grow cuttings. Some gardeners prefer to immerse the cuttings themselves in warm water at this same temperature and then to strike them in the No-Soil compost.

In the case of phlox, cuttings should be taken from washed roots only, for the eel worms live in the stems and leaves and not in the roots. The roots should be washed in running water.

Woodlice. These are sometimes called monkey-bugs, pill-bugs, cheesey-bugs, slaters, etc. They are often abundant in town gardens. They like shady situations and decayed organic matter. They usually hide away in the daytime in crevices in brickwork, on the edgings of paths and under heaps of leaves, etc.

CONTROL. Dust along the edges of paths, the sides of walls

and anywhere it is thought woodlice may hide, with a Derris and Pyrethrum dust.

Fresh powder dusted on after dark when the creatures are moving about will kill hundreds.

Millipedes. Millipedes must be distinguished from centipedes for the former are harmful and the latter beneficial. Millipedes, when babies, are white; when a little older are often grey and when fully grown may be yellowish brown. They are slow to move whereas centipedes move quickly. They have 2 pairs of legs to each segment of their body whereas centipedes only have one pair of legs to each segment, and their bodies are rounded. Millipedes will feed on seedlings, underground stems and roots; they will burrow into bulbs, corms and tubers, and they are a great nuisance because their nibblings may cause an entry for the invasion of fungus diseases.

CONTROL. Fork whizzed naphthalene into the ground at 3 oz to the sq. yard when preparing the soil, if millepedes have been bad in the past. If you incorporate this into the top 2-3 inches of soil it will usually act as a repellant for some months.

Aphides. There are a large number of green flies, blue flies, black flies – plant lice as they are often called – which attack all kinds of flowering plants.

CONTROL. The best way of controlling these pests is to use a good Derris wash or it is possible to make up your own nicotine wash by dissolving $\frac{1}{4}$ oz of nicotine liquid (obtainable from the chemist on signing the poison book), 2 oz of a liquid detergent to $2\frac{1}{2}$ gallons of water. You can of course use half the quantity.

Leather Jackets. These are the larvae of the daddy-longlegs and in the north they are called bots. They feed on all parts of plants growing underground – roots, tubers, corms and so on. They sometimes do harm to herbaceous borders. They may feed throughout the winter; they are usually $1\frac{1}{2}$ inches long and of greyish brown or blackish colour. They are legless and have a tough leathery skin.

CONTROL. A Gamma Dust when applied all over the soil and forked in will kill the leather jackets. I do not like using a Gamma Dust, but as yet have found no other good method of control. I would never use it in the vegetable garden however.

Club Root. This disease is sometimes known as finger and toe and will attack the roots of any member of the cruciferae family. It often gives great trouble with wallflowers, stocks, and annuals like Virginia stock. Roots of affected plants swell and when broken open will be found to contain rotten, evil-smelling material. The plants will be dwarfed and look sickly.

The Virus Problem. It is very difficult to describe virus diseases. They attack flowering plants in different ways. There is what is called Break in tulips, where the colour of the flowers is broken up. There is Yellow Strip in narcissus. There is Stripe in irises. There is the dreaded Spotted Wilt which will attack chrysanthemums, asters, zinnias and so on. In this case you get a kind of spotted depression on the leaves, and the plants, if badly attacked, wilt and look miserable.

A virus is said to be a crystallized protein which is injected as it were into the plant by one of the sucking insects like the Green Fly (Aphides), Capsid Bugs (Tarnished plant bugs) and maybe Thrips. The disease is thus transmitted from one plant to another and the infection will spread extraordinarily quickly. The infection may cause dwarfing, distortion. It sometimes causes blotching of the flowers and foliage and sometimes yellowing of the tips of the foliage.

CONTROL. No definite cure is known. The only thing to do is :

(1) Compost the infected plants properly.
(2) Always start with virus-free material from reliable nurserymen.
(3) Keep down sucking pests by spraying regularly with a good nicotine wash.

Growing healthy plants in plenty of humus always helps matters. The great thing is to keep the plants happy and resistant to disease by seeing that plenty of well-rotted vegetable refuse is incorporated into the ground year by year.

Cuckoo Spit. Most people know this spittle-like deposit on plants. A green bug is found inside, sucking the sap, and causing the shoots to wilt.

CONTROL. Spray with a pyrethrum wash.

Caterpillars.

1. ANGLE SHADES MOTH CATERPILLAR. This moth when resting on a tree or on foliage folds its wings into its body

and simply looks like a crumpled decaying leaf.

The young caterpillars are olive-green in colour, or sometimes brownish, and fed on the leaves of flower buds and on open blossoms. They attack plants both out of doors and under glass.

CONTROL. Spray directly the caterpillars are seen with a pyrethrum wash like Pysect, giving a thorough soaking.

2. SWIFT MOTH CATERPILLAR. The white active larvae of the moths live in the soil and may feed on the herbaceous plants, strawberries, vegetable crops, bulbs, corms, tubers and rhizomes.

CONTROL. Hoe the ground regularly and fork in whizzed napthalene at 3 oz per sq. yard during soil preparation.

3. TORTRIX MOTH CATERPILLARS. These attack herbaceous plants, especially phlox, solidago, heleniums and rudbeckias. These caterpillars draw together two or three leaves of a plant, fastening them with silk-like threads. They may be olive or greyish green.

CONTROL. Spray with liquid derris, and, if possible, handpick and burn all affected shoots and leaves.

Pests of Individual Flowers

Alyssum. FLEA BEETLES. A tiny metallic-like beetle which attacks plants in their seedling stage. They also attack vegetables.

CONTROL. Dust regularly with derris dust – it is a good thing to begin doing this even before the plants come through.

Auricula. ROOT APHIS. Foliage turns yellow and wilts right around the stems where they join the root.

CONTROL. Lift plants, wash roots in a nicotine wash (usual formula). Dip whole plant in this solution for two minutes. Remove soil around plant and replace with sterilized soil.

Lupins. WEEVIL. A grey insect that eats crescent-shaped pieces out of leaves.

CONTROL. Dust with derris at night time. Give young seedlings a feed of dried blood at 1 oz to the sq. yard.

Narcissus. NARCISSUS FLIES. These lay their eggs on the neck of the bulbs in May. Maggots emerge and burrow down to the centre of the bulb. Leaves turn yellow at the tips.

CONTROL. Sterilize bulbs in warm water, as advised on page 180.

Phlox. EEL WORM.

CONTROL. Take root cuttings from tap running washed

roots *only*, as the eelworm lives in the stems and leaves.

Rose. RED BUD BORER. Midge appears from mid July to mid August and lays eggs in wounds made during budding.

CONTROL. Smear buds and raffia with Vaseline directly after budding.

CATERPILLARS AND MAGGOTS. The larvae of many moths attacks the leaves and buds of roses.

CONTROL. Spray with good liquid derris.

SAWFLIES. Various sawflies attack rose leaves, some boring into the stems, some skeletonizing the leaves and others rolling up the leaves.

CONTROL. Spray again with Pyrethrum such as Pysect. Hand-pick and burn all affected leaves and cut off branches tunnelled.

SCALE. The stems of the bushes become covered with round, flat, whitish scales.

CONTROL. Spray well in September and again in February with a white oil emulsion to which a little nicotine has been added.

WEEVIL. A clay-coloured insect particularly destructive to rambler roses.

CONTROL. Place a white cloth under the attacked bush after dark. Shake the bush and flash a bright light on to it. The weevils then fall off and may be collected and burnt.

Stocks. SAWFLY. Little yellowish-green caterpillars collect on the undersides of the leaves and devour them.

CONTROL. Spray with liquid derris immediately the pest is seen.

Violets. RED SPIDER. One of the worst diseases of violets.

CONTROL. Keep soil in frames moist. Syringe the plants daily if enclosed. Dry conditions encourage red spiders. Spray with clean water using, if possible, 100 lb pressure per sq. inch. A derris spray has also proved effective, if a thorough soaking is given.

Diseases of Individual Flowers

Anemone. STEM ROT. Attacks the tuberous roots of the plants causing them to rot. They are waxy when cut.

CONTROL. Dig up and burn.

CLUSTER CUP. Attacks the leaves and stalks forming spots on them from which cup-like fruiting bodies are produced later.

CONTROL. Remove and burn.

Antirrhinum. LEAF SPOT. Attacks the leaves and stems, causing pale brown or whitish spot.

CONTROL. Spray with Bordeaux Mixture (usual formula).

RUST. Rusty brown patches on the undersides of the leaves. Spreads very rapidly.

CONTROL. Give ample room between the plants for circulation of air. Stagnant water-laden air encourages the disease. See that the beds are well drained. Avoid watering the foliage. Don't leave the plants in the ground in the winter. Dust with sulphur or spray with one of the sulphur sprays at intervals.

Aquilegia. STALK AND BULB ROT. A water-soaked spot appears on the stem, the leaves wither and die off.

CONTROL. Remove and compost properly the diseased plants. Dig the bed deeply.

Arabis. WHITE RUST. Appears as shiny raised white patches. Not generally severe.

CONTROL. Dust with a fine sulphur dust. Remove diseased flowers.

GREY MOULD. Appears in patches on the leaves – pale in colour at first, turning darker later.

CONTROL. Dust with a fine sulphur dust.

Michaelmas Daisy (*Aster*). WILT. Enters through damaged portion of the plant. Leaves yellow and mottle in the summer, followed by complete browning when the whole shoot dies.

CONTROL. Do not propagate unhealthy plants. Select clean shoots and take cuttings from them.

STEM ROT. Leaves and flowers hang down and become yellowish-green, later die off. The stem goes black.

CONTROL. Do not over-manure the border; give dressings of lime at 5-6 oz per sq. yard once a year. Remove attacked plants.

Carnations. RUST. Can be a serious disease of carnations, especially in a wet season. Yellowish-brown cushions appear on the leaves.

CONTROL. Pick off infected leaves. Have plants in a well-drained sunny spot. Do not splash leaves when watering. Spray with Captan.

LEAF SPOT. Spots formed on leaves, often with black centres.

CONTROL. As for Rust above.

DIE-BACK AND WILT. More prevalent under glass than in the garden.

CONTROL. Do not grow carnations again in the same spot, and propagate from healthy plants.

Chrysanthemums. MILDEW. White, powdery patches may be seen towards the end of the season on the leaves.

CONTROL. Spray with a colloidal sulphur wash when first noticed.

RUST. Most varieties are attacked by this trouble. Rusty red spots are seen on the under surfaces of the leaves. Usually worse in dry seasons.

CONTROL. Watch out for rusty patches and spray at once with Captan. Burn all old infected plants.

LEAF SPOT. Dark brown patches appear on the upper surface of the leaves.

CONTROL. Compost properly badly affected plants and spray others with Bordeaux mixture.

Dahlia. WILT. This disease causes the whole plant to wilt.

CONTROL. Badly affected plants should be dug up and burnt. Any raspberry canes in the garden should be watched, and if they become affected they too should be dug up and burnt.

CROWN GALL. Large gall-like growths appear in the base of the stalk.

CONTROL. Destroy affected plants. Plant clean in another part of the garden.

LEAF SPOT. Usually appears late in the season. Light yellowish spots appear, later turning greyish-brown, from the middle. Dead tissues fall off. Disease lives through the winter in sticks or dead wood stored with the tubers.

CONTROL. Plant out early in open situation. Spray attacked plants with Captan. Remove leaves in autumn. Plant least susceptible varieties.

DRY ROT. Dry, unsuitable storage places seem to encourage this trouble.

CONTROL. Dig up tubers before first frost. Stand upside down for several days to drain thoroughly. Protect from frost. Dust tubers with equal parts of sulphur and hydrated lime when storing. Disinfect storage place with a 2 per cent solution of formaldehyde.

Delphinium. BACTERIAL SPOT. Deep black irregular-shaped spots appear on both sides of the leaves. Stalks may be affected, also seeds.

CONTROL. Collect and burn all diseased foliage. Spray

regularly with Captan. In severe attacks cut down plants and burn.

MILDEW. White flower-like dust is found on the leaves, stalks and blossoms. The leaves die off prematurely and the buds dry up. In severe attacks the whole plant is stunted.

CONTROL. Avoid over-manuring with nitrogenous matter. Give plenty of space between the plants. Spray with Captan in warm, sunny weather.

Gladioli. BASE DECAY. Reddish-brown raised spots appear on the leaves towards the base. These increase in size and may become black and pitted.

CONTROL. Destroy all diseased leaves by burning. Do not plant corms in heavy, wet soil. Only store healthy corms.

SMUT. Black cushions appear on the corms, leaves and stalks. Corms become completely destroyed.

CONTROL. Remove and burn all infected plants. Dig deeply, lime heavily.

DRY ROT. Corms will split and dry sunken spots appear, reddish-brown in colour. Leaves in spring turn yellow. Stems decay at soil level.

CONTROL. Buy good clean corms. Remove scales and look for sunken spots.

HARD ROT. Yellow patches, later turning brown, appear on the leaves. Dark hard spots appear on the corms. Fungus lives in the soil for four years.

CONTROL. Do not plant in infected soil. Reject infected corms.

Iris. RHIZOME ROT. The rhizomes become soft, putrid and evil-smelling. Base of leaves rot away.

CONTROL. Do not apply lime as alkaline soil encourages the trouble. Burn all badly diseased specimens. Cut diseased portions from very slightly attacked plants and wash in a 2 per cent solution of formaldehyde. Replant in new or sterilized soil.

LEAF SPOT. Yellowish-brown spots and stripes appear on the leaves in autumn.

CONTROL. Spray with lime-sulphur 1 pint to 100 pints of water, three or four times during the summer.

Lily of the Valley. BOTRYTIS. Leaves wilt and turn brown.

CONTROL. Do not grow on infected soil. See that the trouble is controlled on pæonies and it then seldom attacks lilies of the valley.

Lilies. LEAF SPOT. Reddish-brown spots appear on the leaves. Leaves will die, stem may dry up and flowers may be distorted. Trouble spreads rapidly.

CONTROL. Spray with colloidal sulphur two or three times at weekly intervals. In severe cases give the surface of the soil a good soaking with Captan and spray the young growths when they first appear in the spring. Plant bulbs on well-drained soil.

MOSAIC. Leaves become mottled and distorted and petals remain closed.

CONTROL. No known cure. Infected plants must be burned.

Lupins. ROOT ROT. Attacks the roots of the plants, turning them black.

CONTROL. Do not add lime to the soil as this seems to encourage the trouble. Do not plant lupins on the same soil for four years.

Mignonette. LEAF SPOT. Brown patches appear on the leaves. Usually found on plants grown on damp soil deficient in lime.

CONTROL. Spray with Karathane. Give the soil a dressing of hydrated lime.

Roses. BLACK SPOT. Dark spots appear on leaves and young stems. The whole bush may lose its leaves.

CONTROL. Spray with Captan directly spots are seen. Repeat the spray in 14 days. Spray next season as soon as young leaves are developed. Rake up infected leaves and compost them. Mulch the ground with sedge peat one inch deep to prevent the spores blowing up from the soil.

MILDEW. White powdery mildew will be found on the leaves, stems and thorns. The flower bud may also be attacked.

CONTROL. Spray with Karathane. See that the soil gets a good dressing of potash in the form of wood ashes at 8 oz to the sq. yard.

RUST. Orange spots may appear on the under surface of the leaves. Leaves may fall in bad attacks.

CONTROL. Cut out diseased stems immediately they are seen. Spray leaves thoroughly with Captan.

Sweet Peas. STEM ROT. Severe in wet seasons. Lower part of stem turns brown and rots off. Leaves turn yellow and wilt.

CONTROL. Avoid planting on infected ground. Apply wood ashes at 8 oz to the sq. yard.

STREAK. Long brown streaks found on stems and foliage.

Plant looks sickly and very few flowers are produced.

CONTROL. Apply wood ashes at ½ lb to the sq. yard.

Sweet Williams. RUST. Reddish spots on the leaves.

CONTROL. Spray with Captan. Darker varieties seem to be more resistant to the disease.

Tulip. FIRE. Scorched spots appear on leaves and stems. Pitted spots appear on the flowers.

CONTROL. Sterilize affected bulbs with formaldehyde. Immerse for 15 minutes in a 0.5 solution, i.e. 1 pint in 2½ gallons. Spray with Captan when tulips come through ground, again 10 days later and again 10 days after that.

BREAKING. Plant loses vigour and produces small blooms. Foliage is usually mottled.

CONTROL. Keep down insect pests, particularly aphides by spraying with liquid derris.

Violets. May be attacked by Smut, Rust, Leaf Spot and White Spot but none of these are very serious on cultivated violets and the best control in each case is to pick off the affected leaves and burn them and to spray with Captan.

Formulas of Insecticides and Fungicides

Contact Sprays.

NICOTINE AND SOFT SOAP. ¼ oz of nicotine (95.98%) and 2 oz of a clear liquid detergent to 2½ gallons of water.

LIQUID DERRIS. Buy the best types of this non-poisonous paralyzing agent and use according to the instructions on the container.

PYRETHRUM. The extract from the Pyrethrum flower, usually sold as Pysect.

Dust.

DERRIS DUST. Similar to a derris spray but not quite so effective.

Fungicides.

LIME SULPHUR. A brownish red liquid. Purchase it with a polysulphide content of 25 per cent and a specific gravity of 1.30. Never mix with soap.

BORDEAUX MIXTURE. 2 lb of quicklime and 3 lb of copper sulphate to 50 gallons of water.

Mix the copper sulphate in water overnight in a wooden bucket or enamelled container. Slake the quicklime gradually with a little water and then add the rest of the water. Pour in the solution of copper sulphate and stir.

N.B. It is possible to buy Bordeaux in a paste and as this dissolves easily in water many gardeners prefer it.

LIVER OF SULPHUR. 5 oz of liver of sulphur and $\frac{1}{2}$ lb of soap to 10 gallons of water.

KARATHANE gives good control of the fungus diseases known as mildew.

CAPTAN has given good results in the control of Scab, Black Spot and Rust.

The 'Incompletely Safe' Fungicides (CAPTAN AND KARATHANE). Mr. Dunstan Ingle reports : 'Reading the extracts from the official literature, gardeners will see that both the fungicides are not *entirely* free from danger to human beings and animals. Admittedly they are of comparatively low toxicity, but they cannot be recommended *completely* safe for those who are very diligent organic growers. Captan is a good fungicide for the black spots like Black Spot on roses, and Rust on celery. Karathane has proved a good control of the Mildews.

Captan is of low toxicity to warm-blooded animals. May cause skin irritation. Is harmful to fish. May taint fruit for canning or quick freezing. Karathane can be irritating to skin, eyes and nose. Minimum interval to be observed between last application and harvesting edible crops – one week. Dangerous to fish.'

Appendix

Sterilization

The Simple Copper and Bucket Method.

Take an ordinary bucket and perforate all over with holes about 2 in. apart, fill with dry sifted loam. Place a fair sized potato in the middle. Hang bucket about 2 in. above water in a domestic boiler. Turn heat full on and when potato is cooked the soil will be sterilized.

Index

Figures in italics refer to illustration pages.